# How to Fight Fat with Food

## A guide to being slim through healthy eating

# PAUL CHISLETT

# How To
# Fight Fat
# With Food

**Copyright © 2002 by Paul Chislett**

Published by
Chislett Publishing Company
ISBN 0-9542438-0-3

To my best friend and soulmate Samantha.

I am indebted to you for all your continuous support throughout the writing of this book. I could not have done it without you. Thank you.


To my good friend Joan.

My sincere gratitude for all your invaluable help. This book would have been very difficult to complete without you. Thankyou for all that you have done.

# CONTENTS

# INTRODUCTION

The aim of this book is to bring to your attention reasons why an individual may become overweight. It looks at the psychological aspects as well as the physical ones. It will help you to understand yourself more fully and to overcome the different problems related to this condition.

This book will enable you to incorporate a practical, healthy and tasty meal plan into your daily routine, so you not only lose weight, but keep if off!

It does not focus on cutting down the amount of food you eat, rather your toxic and fat intake. The result of which will be a healthier, slimmer, more active body. You will not be hungry on the meal plans that this book suggests, therefore making it easier to sustain. Furthermore, this book is written in a simplistic, no-nonsense manner, enabling you to understand the so-called complicated aspects of the human body with regard to diet and nutrition.

Paul Chislett has lived on many so called 'extreme' lifestyles including vegetarianism, vegan (no dairy products), raw foods, fruitarianism and fasting. He has participated in many kinds of physical exercise since the age of thirteen. Boxing, running (including two London Marathons), weight training, Yoga, Tai Chi and martial arts to name a few.

Paul maintains that poor health and overweight problems are due to our lack of awareness of what we are eating on a daily basis.

The following pages will teach you to become more aware and help you to change your outlook on food. Read each page being careful not to miss out any part. In this way you can be sure of a safe and permanent reduction in weight. Good luck!

# CHAPTER 1

# WHY PEOPLE ARE OVERWEIGHT

People are overweight for various reasons. Some are unhappy, therefore comfort eat. Some people are bored and so it is much easier to go and have a nice cheese and pickle sandwich than to do something else that doesn't involve food. Some just love their food and don't really care about being overweight. Although I personally think that most people that are overweight are very aware of it. They try to make light of it but deep down don't really know how to go about losing it, or they have tried and failed, thus losing the heart to carry on. Some people just can't bare the thought of not having the food that they love to eat for the rest of their lives. Others go on strict diets and then have massive cravings and binge, putting everything back on that they worked hard to lose.

I blame society as a whole, due to our accelerated lifestyles and need for faster foods. But what can be faster than an apple, orange or banana. It comes down to whether or not you are prepared to make a change to your eating regime. It will take discipline, motivation and above all, desire to change. It is down to you.

The comfort eater is probably the most common of all overweight people. In fact, all the other reasons related to excess weight are part of this main problem.

9

Unhappiness for any reason, boredom, lack of confidence or lack of control in our lives are all reasons to eat to comfort our emotions. This usually results in eating far too much food.

It wouldn't be half as bad if we were to eat the right food. Unfortunately, we don't and overweight and unhealthy bodies with systems clogged up with toxins, mucus and fat deposits are the result.

How many cups of tea or coffee are consumed by the average man or woman a day? I'll take a rough guess and say 3-7 cups. Multiply that by 1-3 spoonfuls of sugar, plus milk, which more than likely won't be skimmed, and you can see the excessive amounts of fat and sugar that are being consumed. In addition to that, tea and coffee both contain caffeine, which is a stimulant. It may cause insomnia, induce migraine, tremors and palpitations. It can also accelerate the loss of minerals from bone. It can be addictive and may cause withdrawal symptoms. Tea is known to decrease the absorption of iron from food and may cause gastric irritation.

As you can see, drinking tea and coffee not only adds to the waistline, but to the poor health of the body too. The interesting thing is that we drink when we aren't even thirsty. We are creatures of habit and tea and coffee drinking is a habit that most of us are subject to. Unfortunately, it's an unhealthy one. We must learn to break these habits! Eating habits included!

Social eating is another problem for the person who wants to lose weight. Everywhere we go people are eating the very foods that we are trying not to. "Go on, have another cheese sandwich". It's very difficult and very tiring to keep explaining yourself, especially if you are changing your diet purely for health reasons. You must learn to be disciplined and don't be tempted or swayed by other people's influence, either at work, home or when socialising. Don't be put under pressure, stand your ground.

The slow metabolism is another causative factor of excessive weight gain. To understand it, we need to explain it in a little more detail.

All the food that has been digested moves around our body via the blood. From our digestive system it is taken to the liver. This is where all the good stuff from our food gets sorted out from the bad stuff. The good stuff being usable nutrients and the bad, being in the form of anything unusual or harmful to the body. This can be toxins, colours, preservatives, drugs, environmental pollutants and even cancer cells.

Through a complex system, the liver is able to neutralise these substances and pass them onto the kidneys for elimination. Unfortunately, these harmful substances must be made water-soluble before being exited via the kidneys and many cannot. For those that can't, the next available method is to dissolve them in fat. The liver secretes bile, which it uses to carry the unwanted substances into the digestive system once again for elimination via the stool. Unfortunately, this is not a very efficient method and as a result the uneliminated substances go back into the circulation where they may build up in the system. This obviously may be harmful to the body.

In addition to this, the liver is constantly working overtime, trying to eliminate unwanted substances that we continuously eat. This puts a strain on the liver and over time weakens it, potentially causing liver disorders. This almost certainly slows down your liver's metabolism.

The point is, when the liver is unable to cope, fat-soluble substances go into storage to be dealt with at a later date. The storage is - you guessed it, body fat!

So body fat can, and often is, due to excessive amounts of toxins that have not been eliminated. Due to either the system being overloaded or an individual whose capacity to deal with the toxins is inefficient. This could be due to a person's lifestyle or through liver damage. It may even be due to the fact that the individual just doesn't have a big enough liver to deal with their body weight. For these people, the toxins with which they can't cope, will damage their liver over time. This will obviously add to the problem.

The see-saw dieter, who diets then binges in a repetitive cycle, losing weight only to gain it continuously, puts a tremendous strain on their liver. Their decreased metabolic capacity increases the potential for weight gain in the form of toxic adipose tissue or body fat. If these people continue to diet, their livers will become less and less efficient at coping with toxins.

This all means that many people's weight problems are due to weak livers and/or too much toxin consumption from food additives, drugs and pollution.

This is probably the reason why you just cannot seem to lose weight, even if you don't seem to eat much, because the fat on your body may and probably does contain many toxins that the potentially weak liver cannot shift. Fortunately, the liver has the capacity to rebuild itself. This will be discussed further in Chapter 3.

Drugs, both medical and recreational can cause weight gain. There are many different types of medicines in use today, a large proportion of which contribute to excess weight. Most everybody is aware that the contraceptive pill can and usually does make you overweight. It can induce many changes in liver function. One important effect is to slow down the action of one of the main detoxifying enzymes by as much as a third. Slow liver function has been demonstrated in overweight women taking the pill.

There are also drugs for hormone replacement, diabetes, migraine, heart disease, high blood pressure, anti-inflammatory and antihistamines to name but a few. Many of these may cause weight gain.

Of the recreational drugs, cannabis is the one most associated with weight gain, as it increases the appetite. This is beneficial if you are underweight, but unhelpful if you suffer from overweight problems. All recreational drugs should be left alone, as they intoxicate and interfere with the natural workings of the body.

Most people do not think of medicines as poisons. We tend to concentrate only on their beneficial aspects. We seem to forget that there is no such thing as a safe drug. Do not forget, drugs are nearly always chemicals, which are foreign to the human body and are regarded as such by our metabolic processes.

# CHAPTER 2

# REASONS FOR LOSING WEIGHT

Whatever your reasons for losing weight might be, it can only be of benefit to you. Here are some possible benefits and reasons to start changing your diet.

- Appearance
- Health
- Increased mobility
- Less breathless
- Less lethargic
- Increased vitality (more active)
- Better skin and hair condition
- Enhanced mental clarity
- Sense of achievement

## Appearance

If you want to lose weight due to your appearance, that's fine and is as good a reason as any, but that's only a small percentage of the many benefits that can be experienced with a change of diet. Let's take a look at the others.

## Health

Small changes in your eating habits can lead to big changes in your health. What you eat not only affects your everyday health, but also lays the foundation for the quality of your life and even how long you might live.

Health is, without a doubt, our most valued commodity in life. Ill health not only brings discomfort and worthlessness, but we also become a burden to others.

I personally know people that would not think twice about spending fifty to a hundred pounds up the pub, or thirty to fifty pounds a week on cigarettes, week in, week out, yet the mention of health food is beyond their budget. It's their choice and their money and that's fine. All I'm saying is, try to get things into perspective a little. Think about your body, you only have one. As the old saying goes, "you are what you eat". Eat for health and the other benefits will naturally follow.

### Increased Mobility

As you begin to eat healthier, your weight will naturally reduce. You will be lighter and slimmer, therefore finding it easier to get around. Being able to do little jobs that are now a burden to you will become a pleasure. The excess weight that you are now carrying around will fall away, leaving you free to move in ways that you had forgotten or never before experienced.

Stress on joints is another concern to the overweight man or woman. The heavier you are, the more pressure there will be on your lower back, hip, knee and ankle joints. These areas will benefit greatly from weight loss and therefore the possibility of arthritis and joint pain will be significantly reduced.

## Shortness of Breath and Lethargy

The more weight you are carrying, the more tiring to your system it will be. Weight puts a strain on your whole body. If I were to carry a rucksack on my back with 10-30 pounds of rocks, along with weights strapped to my legs, arms and stomach and tried to lead a normal life, I would soon become very tired. Under such extreme conditions, the lungs and heart are being forced to work overtime.

In the short term, this means shortness of breath and lethargy. The long term effects can be disastrous. Losing weight has obvious advantages.

## Increased Vitality

If you are overweight, it stands to reason that you are not in an ideal state of physical health. Your body will almost definitely be harbouring toxins, fat deposits and mucus through years of eating an incorrect diet. This is also the case of the average man or woman, overweight or not! These toxins etc. clog up your system and inhibit, to a more or lesser degree, the circulation of blood and thus prevent it from carrying out its vital functions. This will most certainly affect your vitality. A healthier blood supply to the internal organs, glands and systems of your body will undoubtedly increase vitality and energy levels, bringing to you an enhanced feeling of well being and happiness.

Some of the main functions of blood are listed below.

## Blood

1.   Transportation of oxygen from the lungs to the cells.

2.   Transportation of absorbed nutrients to the cells.

3.   Conveyance of metabolic wastes from the cells to the organs of excretion, i.e. kidneys, lungs, liver and skin respectively.

4.   Distribution of hormones and other substances that regulate many bodily activities.

## Skin and Hair

A loss of weight and an increase in your nutrient intake will, over time, improve your blood quality and overall health. This will manifest itself through your skin and hair as they begin to take on a healthier appearance.

## Enhanced Mental Clarity

This is another one of the benefits to be experienced when your blood and body become healthier due to a decrease in toxins and fat, and an increase in nutrients, through healthier, more natural foods. A body full of toxins but deficient in nutrients cannot possibly feed the brain with the necessary requirements for clear thinking. Eat natural foods and you will not only lose weight, but will start to feel more alive and begin to think clearer too.

## Achievement

When you begin to take control of yourself and start learning to be disciplined with your eating habits, you will begin to feel good about yourself. Though many dieters know how to lose weight, keeping it off is a different issue. When you master this, you would have really achieved something that you will greatly benefit from in many ways.

## Food for Thought

There are many reasons why a person may choose to lose weight and many benefits to be gained from that loss, not least of all your health. Overweight people are more likely to suffer from heart disease, diabetes, hypertension, strokes and arthritis. What's more is the fact that these conditions are more difficult to treat if you are overweight. Eat healthier, lose weight and reduce these risks!

# CHAPTER 3

## HOW TO LOSE WEIGHT

There are all kinds of diets available to the "would be" dieter. The word diet, for most people tends to suggest a limited intake of food. In fact, there are many diets that actually use this principle as their main weapon. Missing out meals during the day, to be replaced with a drink of some kind, full of so called vitamins and minerals and everything else that the body apparently needs, including a suppressed appetite. If this works for you, then that is fine, but invariably it isn't too long before the weight starts to go back on due to the dieter falling back on their old eating habits. This happens for various reasons as we have already mentioned in Chapter 1.

The meal plans outlined in Chapter 8 are concerned with your health. As already mentioned, eat for health and the rest will follow. I can hear you saying, "But eating healthy is boring, it doesn't taste very nice or interesting." A lot of this is the crux of the whole problem. You must start thinking about food differently. It is fuel for your body. Of course we want it to taste nice, otherwise we wouldn't be able to eat it, but you must learn that to eat too much incorrect food is detrimental to your health and your waistline.

If you have been used to eating all the 'wrong' types of foods for a considerable length of time, then changing to a cleaner, healthier diet will of course seem boring and tasteless. That is why we are going to introduce the meal plans slowly. In this way your mind and body will have time to adjust. This is not only safer, but also makes the weight loss more permanent due to the fact that your mind and body will have gradually been trained to accept and like these new foods. This will cut down the chances of cravings and big binges and hence potential weight gain. It also makes the transition to a different diet easier for you psychologically. You will find that after a period of time (this can vary from person to person) you will become accustomed to eating healthier and will even enjoy it. Yes, enjoy it!

## Increasing Metabolism

This process will automatically happen as you begin to change your diet to a less toxic one. When you start to eat cleaner, healthier foods, the stress upon your liver is automatically reduced. (*Refer to Chapter 1, Functions of the Liver in Metabolism*). Under healthier eating conditions, the liver is able to regenerate itself, increasing its capacity to handle loads it may need to deal with in the future.

You will be providing these conditions when you begin to eat the meal plans in Chapter 8. Due to a cleaner, less toxic intake of food, your liver will have less work to do, thus giving it the chance to rebuild itself. This prepares it for when you begin to burn your body fat through exercise. This will be discussed later. It is possible that this may take a considerable length of time. It all depends on the condition of your liver. A heavy alcohol drinker will obviously have a more damaged liver than a person who doesn't drink or drinks very little. Fortunately, the liver is able to regenerate itself under such conditions, providing a change of lifestyle has been incorporated. Patience is important.

## Exercise

Exercise burns calories and keeps the body fit and healthy. It exercises the joints and muscles, and helps to keep you loose. It works the heart and lungs and helps to remove toxins from the body that will begin to be released due to the change in diet. The toxins come out in sweat. This is why sweat smells. Exercise not only increases perspiration (sweating) but also blood circulation. In this way the toxins are swiftly carried away to the liver and kidneys for elimination.

There are many types of exercise. You must choose one that suits you best or one that you feel drawn to. Personally, I consider Yoga, Tai Chi or Martial Arts some of the best forms of exercise. These disciplines have many breathing exercises as well as their different stretching techniques. This all aids toxin elimination through increased perspiration and blood circulation. Many books on these subjects are available in bookstores and libraries.

Swimming is another very beneficial exercise, especially to the overweight individual, as it not only exercises the lungs and heart, but also keeps pressure off of the joints. It keeps all the joints loose, as well as exercising every muscle group. Cycling is another option and a good one too. Once again, keeping pressure off the joints, but working the lungs and heart. This can also be employed at home whilst watching your favourite soap, with the use of a cycling machine. These are relatively inexpensive when compared to the benefits you may gain, not to mention the convenience of not even having to step outside your front door.

## Caution

Whatever form of exercise you decide to embark upon, caution and patience is of the utmost importance. As you begin to exercise, toxins can be loosened more rapidly through increased blood circulation, as well as fat reduction. The problem is, if you begin to burn this fat through exercise and your liver isn't yet able to cope with the toxins that are stored there, you could be putting your health at risk.

This is why you must detoxify slowly and strengthen your liver's capacity to cope with these toxins continuously for a period of time before beginning any rigorous exercise routines. How long exactly this all takes depends upon many factors. For instance, individual body weights, liver conditions, previous diets including toxin or food additive consumption and individual reactions to a change of diet. Taking all this into consideration, you can see it is impossible to say. It could be weeks, months or in extreme cases, one to two years. Follow the plan correctly and you will not only lose weight safety, surely and permanently, but you will also build a healthier, stronger body.

# Attitude

Your attitude plays a major role in the change of your lifestyle and dietary habits. If you really want to lose weight you must believe in yourself. Are you in control? Do you want to be in control? Some people actually hide behind their obesity. I read somewhere that one woman couldn't lose weight, because she knew her husband felt sorry for her because of her condition. It made her feel important and wanted. She was in control by being overweight. If she lost weight she would lose that control. Fear is a big issue in all our lives. Fear of change, fear of taking control of our lives. Was the lady in question really in control or was she a slave to her own insecurities?

The point is you must be honest with yourself about who you are, even if it hurts. In the long run you will sing for joy due to your new-found freedom, emotional and physical. Though this can take a lifetime of self-evaluation, it all starts by being honest with yourself. Learn to love yourself for who you are. Don't beat yourself up about issues. You are not a saint. You can only do your best.

All this doesn't mean that you should just think, "Oh well, it doesn't really matter then, because I love myself although I am overweight and therefore I will just continue to eat a load of rubbish and treat my body like a rubbish dump". You must find a balance. Yes it would be good if you could love yourself and your body.

Maybe your body is the only thing you don't like about yourself. Then change it! Maybe you do feel ok with yourself, both physically and emotionally. That's great! But making improvements on things that we already feel ok about is great too isn't it? I think yes. What do you think? Because that is what it is all about, what you think and that is what you have to tune into before embarking on a change of lifestyle that will take faith, courage and commitment. Less faith and courage will be needed as you become more experienced about your body and the changes that take place within it.

Commitment will always be required if you want to continue to experience the fruits of your labour. You need to try to cultivate discipline in your life but be gentle with yourself at the same time. Allow yourself time to change. We are all at different stages in our existence and you need to change at your own pace.

Having said all of this, the sooner you set the ball rolling the sooner you will begin to lose weight. Try to remember that food is fuel for your body. You wouldn't drive into a petrol station and put diesel into a petrol-engined car would you? Why not? Because your car would break down wouldn't it? Fortunately for us, our bodies are far more forgiving than man-made machines. Unfortunately, this means we tend to neglect them a great deal.

There are many cars around that you can choose from, plus a whole variety of different forms of transport, but you only have one body, so look after it!

We take it for granted until it breaks down and then complain. Let's change that.

This then is the outline of the plan that we are going to adopt in order for you to lose weight and to maintain that weight loss:

1.	To change your existing diet gradually to a healthier, more nutritious one. This will mean a cleaner, less toxic intake. This in turn allows your body a chance to detoxify or cleanse itself. Initially, this places more stress on the liver due to the extra burden it encounters from the toxins that will be in the bloodstream. We will minimise this by detoxifying very slowly. Detoxification will be discussed further in Chapter 4.

2.	As the stress upon your liver is reduced due to the cleaner intake of food, your liver is able to regenerate itself. The quality of food is an important factor here, as the liver relies on essential nutrients for its regeneration.

3.	Exercise is incorporated into the diet plan to assist in the reduction of your body fat. By this stage your liver would have had time to regenerate, thus increasing its capacity to handle more toxins. Your liver's increased capacity will be needed, when you begin to burn your body fat through exercise, so it is able to cope with the possible toxins stored there.

4.  All these steps require initial motivation from you, as well as commitment and self-belief. If you want to do it you will do. Just remind yourself of the rewards and try to keep positive.

It is extremely important that the plan is followed step by step to allow a safe and permanent weight loss. Do not try to speed up or miss out any part of it, as this may cause unpleasant side effects and be detrimental to your health. In addition to this, if you fail to complete each stage of the plan before moving on to the next, you will find yourself back where you started. As already mentioned, patience is the issue. Do it once and do it right!

While detoxifying and increasing your liver's metabolic capacity, you may find that you do not lose any weight at all. You may even find that you put a little on. Don't worry. This won't last long. It's only a temporary reaction to the increase in food on the new diet plan. It will reverse itself as your liver's metabolic capacity is increased due to the healthier intake of food. Your reaction to the new diet all depends upon your existing body metabolism and the quantity and quality of food you were eating before. Stick with the plan and it won't be long before you notice positive changes to both your physical appearance and energy levels.

# CHAPTER 4

# DETOXIFICATION

Detoxification is a process that your body will go through when you start to change your existing diet to a cleaner, more natural one. It can be an unpleasant experience if it is encouraged too quickly. The most aggressive detox is to not eat at all. In this way, the body starts to cleanse itself quickly. Unfortunately, this would be most dangerous to the average individual who has been eating 'normal' food most of their lives. This is because the toxins and poisons having been loosened rapidly, pour into the bloodstream to be eliminated via the liver and kidneys. The trouble is, the person that has been eating unhealthy foods for years has a lot of toxins in their body. When they are released too quickly as when fasting (not eating at all), they can actually overload the individual's system, causing some very unpleasant experiences. A fast is a wonderful thing if you have eaten yourself into the right condition to embark on one. This takes patience, time and knowledge.

Do not consider fasting until you have read up on this subject and have spent quite some time eating very cleanly (healthy foods). Fasting will be discussed further in Chapter 13.

When you begin to follow the meal plans in Chapter 8, your body will begin to slowly and safely detoxify. You will need to step up your water intake to help carry away the toxins that are slowly being loosened. This will be dealt with more in chapters 8 and 10.

## Why the need to detox?

So your body will be cleaner and hence work more efficiently. Let's go back to our car. You wouldn't drive a car without at least once giving it an oil change would you? If you did, it would be expecting a lot from that vehicle to keep running well and to continue to serve us. Isn't it funny how we expect so much from our bodies and then complain when they break down, or at the very least don't understand why they have broken down.

We need to clean ourselves internally. We spend enough time on our external appearance, yet completely ignore ourselves on the inside. The funny thing is, if we were cleaner internally, we wouldn't need to spend so much time on our appearance. Our inner health would radiate through our entire body and manifest itself on our exterior, making us look younger and feel more energetic. Just take a look at a young child's face. Health isn't just youth, it's a clean body on the inside. That's why you are so healthy when you are young, because you are clean internally, free of all unwanted materials and toxins created by a lifetime of wrong eating.

The need to detox in order to lose weight has already been discussed in Chapter 1 and Chapter 3.

## Where do toxins come from?

Everywhere! Food and drink additives, drugs (recreational and medical), pesticides, household cleaners, polishes, sprays, insect repellents, perfumes, deodorisers, office products and car pollution. We bombard our bodies with these substances everyday of our lives. Funny thing is, most of us don't even give it a passing thought.

### Food

Get into the habit of reading the ingredient list on everything that you consume, food or drink. If you aren't already accustomed to doing this, what you will find will amaze you. Even so called healthy brown bread has fat, emulsifiers, preservatives, flour treatment agents and sugar. This is healthy? I think not! You wouldn't eat these substances if somebody offered them to you on a spoon, (except sugar). Yet when disguised in a loaf of so called healthy bread, it all seems ok. What strange creatures we are. We are slaves to our own tongues. These substances have many side effects, not least of which are excess weight problems. They are not fit for human consumption and therefore should not be eaten.

Nearly all foods in our supermarkets contain such substances and should be discarded from our diet. This includes all drinks that aren't natural fruit juices or water. What you can eat or drink will be dealt with fully in Chapter 8.

# Drugs and Medicines

Nowadays people take tablets like sweets. Any little ailment, cough or headache, we go straight to the doctor. What does he do? Prescribe painkillers, anti-histamines, antibiotics or sleeping tablets to name but a few. Of course, there are situations where certain drugs are essential, but on the whole, many people in my opinion, take more tablets than is absolutely necessary. They become dependant on them. The point is that all these drugs should not actually be in our system. They may help us in certain situations but the side effects these drugs have on our bodies certainly outweigh the positive aspects. Of course, there are times when some drugs can actually save lives and this is a good thing. All I am saying is, if you take tablets every time you have a cold or a headache or you can't sleep, you are overloading your system and the need to detoxify is increased.

Recreational drugs also overload the system, as well as weakening the nervous system and injuring our internal organs. They should be left alone.

# Pesticides

Pesticides in and on our food is another problem. The only way to eliminate these substances from our diet is to eat organic produce. Of course this is expensive, but at what price do you put your health? Organic produce is not only free from pesticides, it is also of a higher nutritional value due to the better quality soil. Pesticides interfere with normal bodily functions and wherever possible, commercial produce should be avoided. Fresh fruit and vegetables are a substantial part of the diet plan outlined in this book and if organic produce is not eaten, you should make sure that you wash your fruit and vegetables well.

## Environmental Pollutants

Other intoxicating substances come in the form of household cleaners such as polishes and sprays of various kinds, insect repellents, perfumes, antiperspirants, office products and let us not forget our lovely old car and its wonderful exhaust fumes. All these substances are within our immediate environment. As a result, our lungs are taking in pounds of pollutants and eliminating volumes of toxic gases each minute!

## Cigarettes

It goes without saying, as you already know, smoking is bad for your health. A high risk of lung disease and/or stroke being the most common. Apart from these two major diseases, smoking has a powerful anti-vitamin C effect. This means that smokers have a lower than normal level of vitamin C in their blood. Vitamin C is essential for growth and vital for the formation of collagen. Collagen is a protein that is necessary for healthy bones, teeth, skin, gums, blood capillaries and all connective tissue. Vitamin C is also important for the healing of wounds and fractures. It increases the absorption of iron and helps to excrete toxic minerals such as lead, copper and mercury.

The effect of smoking upon other nutrients is uncertain, but it is thought to have an adverse effect on B vitamins. Smoking inhibits the workings of the pancreas, a gland that is essential in the digestion of food. There is good evidence that smokers often have poor digestion.

Cigarettes nowadays contain many chemicals, all of which your body has to deal with, not least your liver. Nicotine is also a powerful liver poison.

In simple terms, smoking poisons the whole body much in the same way that eating a diet full of additives does. It also deprives the body of oxygen. Oxygen is vital for health and valuable for detoxification. This deprivation of oxygen speeds up the ageing process. You only have to compare the skin of a chronic smoker to that of a non-smoker to see the truth behind what I am saying.

### Give It Up!

There really is no doubt that it is crucial to give up smoking to secure success, least not for your health. If you are a smoker you may already have tried and failed. Does that mean you can't try again? Maybe you haven't tried everything that might help you.

Giving up smoking is no easy task, though many have done so. Firstly, you must decide for *yourself* to stop whatever the reason, be it health, financial or social. It must be your decision to give up. You will never give up smoking for someone else, although a friend of mine gave up because of his children. However, the decision still came from him.

I know an acupuncturist who has told me he has had an 80% success rate with people wanting to give up smoking through acupuncture. Try it, it might help.

Hypnotherapy is another option and a good one, if it works. The point is you'll never know unless you try it.

There are two main points to remember. Firstly, DON'T GIVE UP TRYING. If you fail, you can always try again, so don't be hard on yourself. The second point is that statistically, every cigarette you smoke reduces your life expectancy by approximately five and a half minutes.

If you can't give up or the prospect of it seems daunting, a reduction in cigarette consumption will certainly help. This is especially so when combined with a healthy diet and regular exercise, as outlined in this book.

## The Liver

Our livers are probably the most important organs in detoxification. It takes poisons, neutralises them and stores what it considers to be harmful. It protects us. However, too much incorrect diet for too long is more than our livers can handle. You will see the result of these excesses in the condition of your skin and hair, not to mention weight gain (*refer to Chapter 1 on metabolism*).

As you can see, the need to detoxify is very important, not only in order to lose weight but also from a purely physiological standpoint. If you fail to do so, you are denying your body the only chance it gets to clean itself of today's high pollutant, high food additive lifestyle. You owe it to yourself and your body, so come on, start living cleaner!

# CHAPTER 5

# ORGANIC OR COMMERCIAL?

People often say to me that organic produce should be cheaper because the farmer doesn't have to pay for pesticides, herbicides or chemical fertilisers. It's a good argument on the surface, but they don't realise that organic farmers do not kill all the weeds with one swift spray of a herbicide. Instead, they rely on manual labour to do the weeding, as well as mulching material like bark or wood chippings to keep the weeds down. They have to introduce many different types of flowers and plants that attract certain insects that prey on aphids (black fly). They don't kill every insect in sight with one passing of a pesticide spray. Natural fertilisers also add to the cost, such as manure or mulch. Add to this that crops are smaller, they spoil faster than chemically treated fruit or vegetables, so more has to be abandoned and it's hardly surprising that organic produce is at least twice the price of commercial. I would love to be able to pay the same price for organic produce as I do for commercial, but that's just not possible. At the end of the day you get what you pay for.

There are no hidden costs with organic. Unfortunately with commercial there are many. For instance, chemicals enter the food chain through wildlife. Soil that is not carefully managed can easily be made sterile through years of chemical use. Groundwater pollution from pesticide residue is a big problem in many agricultural areas. Who do you think forfeits the bill for this? Us! Food produced with chemicals is always deficient in nutrients compared with organic, making it bad value for money. Let us not forget, from the point of view of losing weight or keeping healthy, that chemically produced food builds up toxins in our system and can be stored as fat, as well as putting a strain on the liver and the whole system.

During the 1980's, the government banned the use of 11 pesticides capable of causing birth deformities. This was obviously a cause for concern. But what of the chemical fertilisers, pesticides and herbicides that are in use today? I wonder! Apparently, the formulation and application of today's chemicals is now so advanced that the levels of chemical residue in foods are supposedly much lower and therefore less harmful. This may be true to a certain degree but they are still in the food. These are unnatural chemicals that should not be in our body. That is a fact!

Washing your fruit and vegetables properly by soaking them in very warm water, will of course take off from the skins the chemicals on the outside. You may even consider peeling certain fruits and vegetables. Although this helps to reduce your intake of chemicals from commercially produced food, don't be fooled. These chemicals are on the inside of your foods. The leaves of the plants or trees absorb the chemicals as they are sprayed. The chemicals travel through the entire tree and end up in the fruit. Chemical fertilisers are absorbed by the roots of the trees and they too travel to the inside of your fruits and vegetables. This cannot be washed off. It is just another toxin your body has to deal with.

There really is no comparison in taste between commercial and organic produce. This is especially true of fruits. Unfortunately people often buy fruit for looks, not realising that commercial produce has been enhanced chemically using waxes and other such methods. If you were to taste an organic orange or banana against a commercially produced fruit of the same type, I doubt if you would go back to eating commercial. You can taste the greater nutrient content in the flavour of these foods, plus you have the added benefit of keeping your system 'clean', as well as the environmental benefits.

The cost of cigarettes is astronomical, but somehow even people on very low incomes seem to find the money for them. Mention health foods to these people and their reaction is usually, "I can't afford it". Organic is always totally out of the question.

Don't kid yourself that you feel fine or that you don't notice any side effects from food additives or chemically produced food. They are all in your system, slowly taking their toll on you. It's just too subtle for you to notice.

Of course organic produce is expensive and not everyone can afford to eat it all the time. It's a matter of priority. If you really want to lose weight and stay healthy, ideally you should eat organic food as often as possible.

Just remember, the next time you are trying to decide whether or not to pay double for those organic oranges, there is a lot at stake in that decision. Commercial produce is much cheaper short term but in the long run we all end up paying more. Organic on the other hand is more expensive up front, but there are no hidden costs.  The choice is yours.

# CHAPTER 6

# COOKED OR RAW?

By eating a diet high in raw food, you will be consuming food as it was intended by nature. There is little doubt that fruit and vegetables are at their nutritional best in their raw state. They are full of the vitamins, minerals and enzymes that our bodies require for optimum performance. They are the true whole foods.

When you start to bring raw foods into your diet, you will not only be doing away with artificial flavourings, colours and preservatives that are typical of today's convenience foods, but also the most common form of food processing in use today – cooking. This process not only damages the nutritional content of food but also reduces its health rejuvenating properties.

Fruit or vegetables in their natural state are alive. They are living foods that are bursting with 'life force' and life enhancing nutrients. Cooked foods are dead foods. Many of the enzymes, if not all of them, have been destroyed. Enzymes are essential for the absorption of vitamins and minerals. They play a role in boosting the body's detox systems as well as rebuilding damaged cells. Raw foods contain ample supplies of vitamins, minerals and live enzymes, making them the most complete food available to man.

40

Eating raw foods, especially fruits, will make you feel more alive. A new feeling of well being and optimism will begin to generate from within you. It doesn't mean eating tasteless, uncooked food, but rather tasty, nutritious, vibrantly alive food. This will, over time, begin to make you feel more alive, instead of feeling lethargic like you do when eating cooked, dead food.

## Weight Loss

Raw fruits and vegetables are low in fat. As previously mentioned, your toxic intake will also be reduced when consuming these types of foods. This will undoubtedly promote weight loss.

## Types of Raw Food

- Fresh fruits
- Vegetables
- Salad fruits
- Green leaf vegetables
- Sea vegetables
- Herbs
- Sprouted beans and pulses
- Sprouted grains
- Nuts (though too many can be fattening)
- Seeds
- Dried fruits

Of course, the above list may not seem very appealing to you at the moment. Don't worry, you are not going to be eating raw food alone in order to lose weight. However, these foods or some of them, particularly fruits and vegetables, will form a percentage of the meal plans outlined in this book.

More and more people are becoming aware of the need for a more natural way of living and healing. Who had heard of Yoga, Tai Chi, acupuncture or homeopathy fifty years ago? Health stores are everywhere and organic produce is more readily available. This growing awareness is pointing the way forward for science and humans to a more natural diet consisting of whole, living, organic foods, high in vitamins, minerals and live enzymes.

Those who increase the amount of raw living foods in their diet, can expect to see many positive changes in themselves. As your body begins to rejuvenate, you may over time, experience some of, if not many or all of the benefits listed below.

## Benefits

- Increased vitality
- Improved mental clarity
- Improved immunity
- Enhanced enthusiasm for life
- Improved concentration
- Decrease in sleep needs
- Balanced emotions
- Weight loss or gain  - depending on needs
- Softer skin
- Brighter eyes
- Shinier hair
- Stronger nails

Other benefits include:

- Less time cooking
- Less washing up
- Kinder to the environment

I must stress to you at this point not to go straight over to a complete raw food diet, even though I doubt there are too many people that would want to, but just for those individuals that may attempt it, beware. There are many benefits to be gained from a diet high in raw foods, especially fruits, but you must change gradually for reasons already discussed in previous chapters.

# CHAPTER 7

# THE WAY FORWARD

You would have learnt from the previous chapters that excess weight problems are due to a combination of emotional factors, social pressures, habit eating of 'wrong' foods and a slow metabolism due to an overload of toxic substances from your food and environment.

Acceptance of today's society with its food products and all their additives, other people's diets, your own diet and environmental pollution, has all contributed to your overweight condition. You must begin to rebel if you are to lose that weight. Don't accept it for another minute!

This may all seem like circumstances that are beyond your control, but don't despair. You can gain control. You just need motivation and time to change. This needs to be backed up with some good, sound knowledge. The knowledge can be found in this book. The rest is up to you.

As you work through the diet plans, you will be learning a lot about yourself. Individualism is an important factor here. No two people are the same and your reactions to the change of diet may and probably will be totally different to another persons. Success of the diet depends a great deal on you and your ability to interpret the reactions and changes that take place. This is important so you are able to make appropriate dietary changes at various stages of your progress. You will learn through experience.

You must learn to care about yourself enough to make some big changes. Changing your diet doesn't just mean changing what you eat. It means changing your outlook, changing where you shop and possibly even changing your friends if they don't support you. This takes a certain amount of courage, if not a considerable amount. You must not be afraid to go against society's grain. Stand up for yourself and what you believe in. Do it for you. Make that change.

You may feel isolated at first, or completely alone. Don't worry, learn to take it in your stride and remember, it is for you! These negative emotions will begin to fade away as time goes by and you start to see positive changes. Have faith!

Try standing in front of a full-length mirror whilst you are naked. Have a good look at yourself all over. How does it make you feel? What you think or feel may bring to your attention some psychological baggage that you need to overcome before you can successfully overcome your weight problem.

Don't get too bogged down with the psychological aspects of it, rather just have a look and see what comes up. It's all part of the self-development aspect of you. Through this observation of yourself comes knowledge of who you are and what makes you tick. This in turn holds the potential for change (providing you want to) and a stronger individual. As already mentioned, don't get bogged down with this, just have a look at yourself and it will happen naturally. Above all, be honest with yourself.

Learn to appreciate yourself. You can do this by writing affirmations such as "I am the most important thing in my life". Write this down until you truly believe it. It is important that you cultivate self-worth and belief. This will provide you with the strength needed for this journey.

If at any stage you become ill for any reason, you might need to slow the whole process down. You will need to be the judge of this by the way you are feeling at that time, should it occur. Illness puts a strain on the system as it tries to fight off infections. This puts a greater demand on the liver. You will need to put yourself in some kind of a holding regime until the illness has passed.

If you start to feel ill whilst you are on the exercise part of the plan, it maybe an indication that you are pushing yourself too hard. You will need to slow down a little, or stop exercising altogether. Build yourself up and introduce it once again slowly. Listen to your body.

Don't concern yourself with your weight, rather your shape, so put away your scales for now and prepare to embark upon a journey of a lifetime.

# CHAPTER 8

# WHAT TO EAT

By now you will have a pretty good idea of what is required in order for you to lose weight. This chapter provides you with the necessary tools for accomplishing that task. It is the backbone of the whole plan, what you can and can't eat.

I am not going to spend a lot of time talking about what nutrients are in certain foods, I will leave that up to the 'nutrition experts'. However, a good supply of vitamins and minerals is essential in order for you to detoxify and rebuild the liver and the body. In particular, iron, folic acid and vitamin C are of great importance.

Iron is extremely important for effective detoxification. It is used in one of the liver's metabolic cycles. Avoiding tea, coffee and foods with many additives will improve your body's ability to absorb iron. There really is no point in eating foods that contain certain nutrients if we are to undo the good by washing it down with a nice cup of tea. *(Refer to Chapter 1)*.

Folic acid is one of the B group vitamins. It is essential for building new liver tissue and replacing cells throughout the body.

Vitamin C is important for healing, is an ANTIOXIDANT and aids iron absorption from plant food.

## Foods Rich in Iron

| Vegetable Sources | | |
|---|---|---|
| Peas | Parsley | Butter Beans |
| Leeks | Broccoli | Haricot Beans |
| Watercress | Spring Greens | Mung Beans |
| Radishes | Lentils | |

| Fruit Sources | | |
|---|---|---|
| Blackcurrants | Loganberries | Dried Apricots |
| Redcurrants | Prunes | Dried Figs |
| Raspberries | Raisins | |

## Foods Rich in Folic Acid

| Vegetable Sources | | |
|---|---|---|
| Cabbage | Watercress | Spring Onions |
| Broccoli | Lettuce | Sweetcorn |
| Brussels | Spinach | Endive |
| Beetroot | Chicory | |

| Fruit Sources | | |
|---|---|---|
| Avocado | Melons | Oranges |

# Foods Containing Vitamin C

| Vegetable Sources | | |
|---|---|---|
| Potatoes | Asparagus | Beansprouts |
| Brussels | Broccoli | Mustard & Cress |
| Watercress | Cauliflower | Mint |
| Cabbage | Radishes | Parsley |
| Kale | | |

| Fruit Sources | | |
|---|---|---|
| All Berries | Melons | Mangoes |
| Guavas | Blackcurrants | Pineapple |
| All Citrus    -    Oranges etc. | | |

It is important that you eat some of the foods from the above tables every day. Suggested menus can be found towards the end of this chapter

## Objectives

There are two primary objectives of this dietary system. They are:

1.    To reduce as much as possible your toxic and saturated fat intake to an absolute minimum.

2.    To supply your body with the nutrients it requires to rejuvenate and sustain itself.

These two objectives will ultimately result in a safe reduction of excess adipose tissue (fat).

## "Clean Food"

This is food that has been untouched and unpolluted with chemicals during its growth and processing. Eating these foods will ease the load on your detoxifying systems and reduce the chemical level in your blood and tissues. 'Everyday food' is full of additives and finding natural foods means changing your place of purchase. Obviously, the health food shop is a good place to buy such foods and once you start to shop at these places you will find some truly wonderful foods there.

## Additives

As previously mentioned, you must get into the habit of reading the ingredient lists on everything you purchase. This is absolutely crucial to your success. You must reduce your toxic intake to an absolute minimum if you are to lose weight. The sooner you do this, the sooner you will see results. Do not purchase anything that has any additives in whatsoever. There are no exceptions to this rule if you are to be successful. You can purchase a book on 'E' numbers and additives from any good book store, or visit your local library. This will show you just how harmful some of these substances really are. It will also teach you that some additives are of a natural origin. However, I personally believe that any food that has been played around with in any way at all is inferior and potentially harmful to the body. You may draw your own conclusions.

## Shelf Life

Any food that lasts a long time has usually been treated with preservatives. The exceptions to this rule are grains, dried beans and dried fruit. So basically, if you purchase food and it goes bad after a relatively short period, you know it has no preservatives. This is a good rule of thumb to adopt.

## Processed Food

To pick an organic fruit straight from the tree and eat it is to consume food as it was intended, with no artificial processing whatsoever. All confectionery – chocolates and sweets etc, crisps of all kinds, prepared foods, bakery products, biscuits, fast foods and juice drinks (with the exception of natural juices) are all heavily processed and contain many additives in the form of artificial colours, flavourings and preservatives. These foods should be excluded from your diet altogether.

## Bread

Bread is an excellent food. Or at least it should be. It is a good source of starch and protein, is high in fibre and contains B complex vitamins, as well as iron and calcium. Unfortunately, it also contains a lot of additives. Finding additive free bread can be a problem. Try the health food store, as well as your local baker and have a chat with them. A long-standing family baker is your best chance of supplying additive free bread. You may be able to come to an arrangement on a weekly order of such bread made from organic flour.  This will undoubtedly cost more, but you must remind yourself of your objectives.  Of course, we are talking of wholewheat bread here and not its white cousin, which has been through more processing and left deficient in nutrients.  Although in England, all flours, except wholewheat, are required by law to be enriched with the added nutrients thiamine, niacin, calcium and iron, though I don't believe that added nutrients can possibly be as beneficial to you as naturally occurring ones.  White bread is also lacking in fibre, in comparison with wholewheat bread, with 100g of white containing 1.5g of fibre as opposed to 100g of wholewheat containing 5.8g.

## Dairy

You have to ask yourself whether or not dairy is a good thing to consume, or should we really be consuming it at all?  Milk really is for one thing and one thing only, calves!  That's baby cows.  The only time you should drink milk, is when you are a baby and suckling from your mother's breast.  After 2-3 years of age we should discontinue drinking milk of any kind whatsoever.  Why do you think it is, that so many children become lactose intolerant by the age of 3?  Could it possibly be due to the fact that they are not supposed to be drinking it?  I wonder.  Take a look at a cow and compare its size to that of a human.  A young calf needs a high supply of fats and other nutrients to sustain its size, as well as for growth.  It is true that milk does contain essential B vitamins, phosphorus and zinc, and is an excellent source of calcium, as well as providing high quality protein.

Trouble is, it also provides high quality fat, which when you are trying to lose weight is a definitive no no. If you must drink milk, skimmed is the only option if you want to succeed in losing weight. Semi-skimmed is still too high in fat, though it can serve the purpose of a useful transition from full fat milk to skimmed. The vitamins and minerals that milk provides can be found in abundance in many other foods, namely the 'right' foods outlined in this chapter.

## Cheese

Cheese often contains colours and preservatives, as well as being high in fats. It should be avoided altogether, or at least cut your consumption to an absolute minimum. Even then, you should eat low fat or half fat vegetarian cheese. Low fat cottage cheese is another option, but not too much. Be sure it has no additives.

## Margarine or Butter?

This is a big problem area due to people believing that margarine is relatively good for them compared with butter. In one sense it is. Margarine contains less saturated fats than butter and is high in polyunsaturates. Saturated fats occur naturally in meat and dairy products. They have been shown by medical research and population studies to increase blood CHOLESTEROL levels and the risk of coronary heart disease. Polyunsaturated fats on the other hand, are required by the body to produce hormone-like substances that carry out a range of functions, including inflammation control and blood flow. They are needed as part of the make-up of cells and have also been shown to be helpful in the treatment of heart disease, psoriasis and arthritis. You would think that margarines labelled 'high in polyunsaturates' are therefore healthy and good for us. Unfortunately, these soft margarines are highly processed and contain many additives. Butter is a more natural product than margarine but has a higher content of saturated fats. Basically, these products should not be consumed as they are both unhealthy and potentially fattening.

Low fat spreads may still contain many additives and should therefore be avoided. Margarines purchased from the natural health food shop are a much better option and should be used if your desire for margarine is too great. Read the ingredient lists.

Polyunsaturated fats that are found in margarines and useful to the body, may also be found in olive, sunflower, soya bean and rapeseed oils, walnuts and oily fish such as sardines, mackerel and salmon.

## Eggs

Eggs contain a multitude of vitamins and minerals. Sodium, potassium, phosphorus, iron, zinc, sulphur, retinal, niacin, pantothenic acid, biotin, folic acid, vitamin D, vitamin E and vitamin B12 to name but a few. They are also a rich source of protein. The trouble is, they are also high in cholesterol and saturated fats and should eventually be excluded from your diet. However, four to six eggs a week are recommended at this stage. These should be either scrambled or in an omelette to aid digestion. They are permitted irrespective of their fat content, as they contain vitamins and amino acids that are essential to good liver function. You must buy free range though, as they contain a higher nutritional value, as well as being less polluted, tastier and a lot kinder to the bird. Fried eggs are hard to digest and therefore should not be eaten.

All dairy produce is a big contributing factor in excess weight problems. If you were to cut out all your dairy foods, with the exception of the recommended number of eggs a week, you will notice a big difference in a short period of time.

## Meat

Humans were never intended to consume the rotting flesh of a dead animal. We don't have the teeth, the intestines or the stomach acid production to break it down. However, I realise that many of you are not vegetarians and do enjoy eating meat. Eat only white, such as chicken or fish. Red mead has too much fat content and you will not lose weight if you eat it. Stay away from offal (internal organs). The internal organs of animals do the same job as that of humans. They act as filters and all livers and kidneys of intensively reared animals are full of toxins, pesticides and drugs of various kinds. Hearts should also be avoided, as the blood of these animals carries the poisons throughout the body.

Free-range animals and birds are more likely to be free from chemical contamination and therefore chicken, wild duck and rabbit may all be eaten in moderation, boiled or grilled without the skin.

## Fish

Fish is a relatively safe food, as they swim wild and are therefore uncontaminated with chemicals, though they can pick them up from field run-off and industrial chemical pollution. However, fish are high in unsaturated oils or fats. These are not only beneficial to the body, but also far less fattening than saturated fats found in red meat. Avoid farmed fish such as trout or salmon, as they will more than likely be contaminated with chemicals. Fresh caught sea fish is probably the cleanest you will eat in this country. Cod, haddock, sole, skate or herring being the best choice, may be eaten two or three times a week. Do not buy canned or frozen fish, especially fish fingers. They usually contain colourings and other additives. Smoked fish may be coloured with coal-tar dye and should not be eaten. Tuna should also be avoided. They live for 30-40 years, during which time will probably feed in contaminated waters. As a result, they accumulate high levels of toxins and metals in their flesh. The healthiest way to cook fish is to steam, bake or grill it.

## Sugar

This substance is used in foods far too liberally in my opinion. Sucrose (sugar) is over 95% carbohydrate with practically no other nutritional value. It is known to suppress the appetite and cause tooth decay.

One other problem with sugar is the fact that the body tends to dump its molecules into fat. Therefore your sugar intake should be reduced to a bare minimum if you are to lose weight. Sugar is used in many foods as a preservative and a sweetener, so read those ingredient lists and stay away from such foods. No more than two teaspoonfuls per day should be consumed and even then it should be dark brown unrefined or raw cane sugar. Honey may be used as a substitute for sugar but once again, not too much. It is lower in calories than sugar and therefore a good substitute. No more than three teaspoonfuls per day should be consumed.

## Vegetables

Vegetables are a good source of protein and probably the least polluted. Protein is important to good liver function, with peas and beans being valuable sources, as well as whole grains, nuts and seeds. Nuts and seeds are good in salads or for quick snacks. Vegetables provide a wide range of nutrients as well as antioxidants. Broccoli, carrots, tomatoes, kale and red peppers being particularly beneficial in this area, may be eaten as much and as often as you wish.

## Bean Shoots

This is a cheap and easy way to provide you with a good source of easily digested protein. Bean shoots are also low in calories and packed with vitamins, enzymes, minerals and sugars. Mung bean shoots are the most commonly used, especially in Chinese cooking. However, any bean can be sprouted and aduki beans, chickpeas, lentils, alfalfa seeds and soya beans are also used. Soya bean shoots must be cooked before eating though, as they contain toxic proteins, as should chickpeas so they may be tender enough to eat. The only problem with this is many of the nutrients will be destroyed, thereby defeating the object of eating them in the first place. Stick with the other beans and seeds so you may eat them raw or at the very worst lightly fried in a stir-fry. If you want them in a stir-fry, add them at the end of cooking for just a minute or two. Red kidney beans should be thoroughly soaked and boiled before consuming.

To sprout your own beans, all you have to do is select the desired quantity, making sure you have discarded any damaged or discoloured ones. Soak them overnight or for about 12 hours in pre-boiled lukewarm water. Rinse them off and place them in a container such as an old ice-cream carton, leaving enough room between the beans to allow for shoots. Cover the container with a cotton or muslin cloth secured with an elastic band. Place the container in a warm, dark place. Do not allow the beans to dry out. This may be achieved by rinsing them in tepid water 2-3 times a day. Alternatively, the beans may be laid on a cotton or muslin base placed in the container. This can be kept moist by spraying with water daily. Don't over soak. Your shoots will be ready to eat within 2-6 days.

Books on raw foods and sprouting are available if you require more information on this subject. Take a look in your local library, I'm sure you will find something there.

# Guidelines

There are a few basic guidelines that should be adhered to as much as possible when buying food.

1.  Avoid frozen and tinned foods. The farmers are forced to spray these foods more, as the manufacturers demand perfect looking produce.

2.  Peel or scrape potatoes. They are sprayed constantly when growing and are usually treated again once picked to prevent sprouting.

3.  Buy vegetables as fresh as you can. 'New' potatoes and carrots when you have a choice. Don't buy stored produce, as it will more than likely have been sprayed with growth inhibitors.

4.  Always read the ingredient list on everything you purchase. Stay away from anything unnatural. You will come to realise there isn't a lot in 'normal' food stores that doesn't contain additives of some kind. You will need to start buying your food in the health food shop. That doesn't mean you won't need to read the ingredients of what you want to buy. Unnatural substances have a way of getting into our foods no matter where we shop. However, the health food shop is most definitely the wisest choice.

# Rules to be followed

1.  Forget everything and anything you have ever thought about dieting. It will only hinder your progress.

2.  You must make sure that you eat enough food. This is paramount. Your body will be detoxifying and re-building. It must have the necessary nutrients to do it properly. Eat little and often, with three main meals, plus light snacks in between. Never gorge yourself.

3.  Don't allow yourself to get too hungry. If you feel like a nibble, then do so.

4.  Do not concern yourself with the amount of food you will be eating. If you put a little weight on, it will soon come off again if you stick to the rules.

5.  Never eat after 7.00 p.m. and always leave at least two hours after finishing your last meal before retiring to bed. This rule should be applied to exercise also, leaving two hours after eating before commencing any exercise routine.

6.  Study and follow Chapter 10, for the safest and most permanent reduction in weight.

The amount of food you consume at each meal depends on the individual. As already mentioned, don't gorge. You should leave the table feeling satisfied, but not stuffed.

These then are the rules to be adhered to in order to secure success.

I have divided the foods into RIGHT, MAYBE and WRONG. Obviously the RIGHT foods are what you should stick to. The MAYBE foods can be eaten occasionally with caution if need be. The WRONG foods should be avoided altogether. They contain far too many additives of all kinds and will definitely hinder your progress.

# Right Foods - Vegetables

| Vegetables | Quantity | Cooking | Comments |
|---|---|---|---|
| Green leaf salad, lettuce cucumber etc. | As much as you like | Raw | Watercress, especially good for detox. |
| Broccoli, cauliflower, cabbage, kale, brussels | As much as you like | Steamed | Organic where possible |
| Potatoes | 1 medium | Baked, boiled | Organic 'New' |
| Carrots, parsnips, beet, swede, onions, leeks etc. | As much as you like | Baked, boiled, steamed | Organic |
| Peas, green beans | As desired | Lightly boiled | Organic |
| Pulses – lentils, butter beans etc. | 1 cup soaked | Boil well, follow instructions | Chickpeas especially |

# Right Foods - Vegetables

| Vegetables | Quantity | Cooking | Comments |
|---|---|---|---|
| Bean shoots/ sprouts | 1 handful | Stir-fry, raw | Good source of protein and nutrients |

# Right Foods - Fruit

| Fruit | Quantity | Cooking | Comments |
|---|---|---|---|
| Any fresh fruit | 2-5 pieces | Raw, stewed | Soft fruits |
| Fruit spreads, jams etc. | As desired | Pre-made Home-made | Strictly sugar & additive free (health store) |
| Dried fruit | 50-80g 1 handful | Raw, stewed | Un-sulphured only |

# Right Foods - Grains

| Grains | Quantity | Cooking | Comments |
|---|---|---|---|
| Rice | 200-300g (1 cup) | Boiled | Short grain, organic (brown) |
| Rice cakes (without salt) | As desired | Pre-packed | A great snack (health store) |
| Barley | 200-300g (1 cup) | Boiled | Best in soups/ stews |
| Millet | As desired | Boiled | Health store |
| Ryvita (crispbread) | As desired | Pre-packed | A great snack |
| Corn | 1 cup or 1 cob | Boil, steam, bake | As a side dish or starter |
| Cous cous | As desired | Lightly boiled 5-8 minutes | Don't over boil |
| Bread (Whole wheat) | 2 or 3 slices | As purchased, or toast | Sugar/ additive free only (Health store) |
| Pasta | As desired (not too much) | Boiled | Wholewheat, organic |

# Right Foods - Miscellaneous

| Food | Quantity | Cooking | Comments |
|------|----------|---------|----------|
| Fish | Twice weekly | Grill/bake | Fresh, not smoked |
| Eggs | 1 a day (maximum) | Scrambled, poached (not fried) | Free-range |
| Yoghurt | 1 per day – 125g | | Natural live/ goat or sheep's milk |
| Nuts | 50g (max.) per day | Raw | Walnuts, almonds, brazils, cashews |
| Seeds | 50g a day | Raw | Sunflower/ pumpkin – great snack |

# Right Foods - Dressings

| Dressing | Quantity | Cooking | Comments |
|---|---|---|---|
| Tamari (Soya Sauce) | As desired | | Sugar additive free only |
| Lemon juice | As desired | | Fresh squeezed |
| Herbs | As desired | | Purchase book |
| Pepper | As desired | | |
| Oil (Olive) | 1-3 teaspoons | For stir-fries and salads | Extra virgin, cold pressed |
| Miso | 1-2 teaspoons | Add to soups | Health store |

# Maybe Foods

| Food | Quantity | Cooking | Comments |
|------|----------|---------|----------|
| Milk | Half pint a day max. | As required | Skimmed only |
| Cheese | 50g max. 3-4 days | | Low fat vegetarian, goat or sheep's |
| Margarine | Sparingly (not too much) | | Low fat, heath store margarine only, additive free |
| Chicken, turkey | 2 or 3 breasts weekly (remove skin) | Grill, boil, casserole | Free-range (organic preferably) |
| Poultry/ game, pheasant, rabbit | 100g weekly max. | Grill, boil, casserole | Organic |

# Wrong Foods

| Food | Varieties | Comments |
|------|-----------|----------|
| Dairy | Full fat cow's milk, cream, butter, margarine, full fat cheeses | Too much fat and additive content |
| Meat | Beef, pork, bacon, veal, ham, lamb, burgers, sausages, offal | Too much fat. Also pesticide and drug residues |
| Flour products, pastries etc. | White bread, cakes, biscuits, puddings, pies etc. etc. | Contain fats, sugar, additives |
| Confectionery | Chocolate, sweets, desserts, jams | Contain fats, sugar, additives |
| Cereals | All types from supermarkets etc. | Contain sugar and additives |

## Wrong Foods

| Food | Varieties | Comments |
|------|-----------|----------|
| Dressings, sauces etc. | All types including mayonnaise, ketchup and sauces in tins. Pasta sauces, baked beans etc. | Additive and sugar free forms are ok in moderation. Read the ingredient labels (Health store) |

There you have it. What you can and can't eat if you want to lose weight. I realise that on face value it may look a little grim, but you must decide what you want. Some of you will be able to change your diet quicker than others. Some of you having looked at the above information, will even be thinking to yourself, "I can't do it". For those of you that are, try not to be so negative. If the concept of eating the RIGHT foods all the time and nothing else is depressing to you, then read chapters 1-3 again and start to make changes to your existing diet by introducing the RIGHT roods and eliminating the WRONG foods slowly. This can be done at a pace that suits you. You can be the judge.

Once you start to shop at the health food store, you will be surprised at the abundance of natural foods that you are able to eat. A privately owned store will provide you with a larger variety than the well known stores, as it is more important for them to gain your custom. Remember to always read the ingredients on everything you purchase.

Some of the foods that may be obtained there include jams/fruit spreads, dried fruit, rice cakes, loose grains, cereals, wholewheat pasta, natural yoghurts, nuts and seeds, tamari soya sauces, herbs, goat and sheep's milk cheeses, minimally processed margarine, vegetable paté and sprouted wheat loaves to name but a few. All of these foods may be eaten. Some more than others and all in moderation of course. Of the jams, Whole Earth and Meridian I have found to be particularly good. They use natural fruit juices to sweeten them and fruit pectin as a gelling agent. There are other brands available, so have a look. Whole Earth also make organic cereals free of all additives as well as other products.

Beware of sulphur dioxide (E220) in some dried fruits, particularly apricots and apple rings. There are many other dried fruits you can choose from that contain no additives at all. Of the rice cakes, go for the salt free ones. In fact, go for salt free everything. We consume enough salt that occurs naturally in our foods. Why add more than we need? Some rice cakes are sweetened with honey, making them more interesting. Organic wholewheat pasta makes a wonderful meal with vegetables, chickpeas and miso sauce. Miso is a smooth puree made from soya beans, fermented rice or barley and sea salt, which have aged together over a period of several months to several years. It is highly nutritious containing enzymes, protein, vitamins, minerals and complex carbohydrates. It can be used for soups, sauces, gravies and spreads. It should be used in moderation though, due to its high salt content.

Natural yoghurts and even soya yoghurts are also available. Be sure that you only buy those with no added sugar. Vegetable paté may be purchased and can make your snacks a little more interesting. Once again, read the ingredients to be sure. Sprouted wheat loaves are tasty, filling and highly nutritious. They are usually organic too.

A word to those of you who may find giving up tea and coffee a problem. Have a good look at some of the natural beverages. There's a wide choice of herbal teas and cereal drinks made from barley, chicory and/or rye. Dandelion root coffee is a very good coffee substitute and may be used in its place. If you are able to obtain pure dandelion root you'll be able to make an infusion. Dandelion root stimulates the liver and kidneys to release toxins and is high in vitamin A. Vitamin A is particularly important to liver function. This can be part of your overall general health plan. The use of herbs in cooking and their effects can be found in books. Check out the library.

There are just another couple of points to consider. Do not eat fruit as a pudding. Fruit is digested far quicker than other foods and if eaten after a meal, will interfere with digestion. You may eat fruit as a starter and in such cases, allow 20-30 minutes to lapse before eating the main course. In this way the fruit will have been digested before your system is given the chore or breaking down the rest of the meal. Get into this habit and it will serve you well. Try to forget about pudding. It's a tradition that your body can do without.

The other point to remember is to always chew your food well. This will aid digestion through increased saliva production. Saliva contains digestive enzymes and is increased by chewing. Chewing your food to a paste also gives your digestive organs less work to do. Practise this and you will benefit from it more than you realise. Use your teeth for what they are intended.

## Meal Plans

*Suggested Menus*

After rising first thing in the morning, drink a cup of boiled or filtered water with fresh squeezed lemon juice from half a lemon or a whole one if you wish. The water should be allowed to cool if boiled and a teaspoon of honey may also be added for taste. This drink may help to induce a bowel movement and is also a good liver cleanser. Wait at lease 15 minutes before eating breakfast.

You can choose one meal, a, b, c etc. from each time period of the day.

*Breakfast*

a.     Half a grapefruit or other piece of fresh fruit, followed by health store cereal with skimmed milk. No sugar.

b.     3-5 pieces of fresh fruit (not bananas), followed by 1 or 2 pieces of wholemeal toast with honey.

c.     Boiled, poached or scrambled egg on toast. (1 egg, 1 or 2 slices of wholemeal toast).

*Mid-Morning (10-11 a.m.)*

a.     1-3 pieces of fresh fruit.  Not bananas.

b.     Half a banana with natural live yoghurt.

c.     2 or 3 rice cakes with health store vegetable paté, miso or humus.

*Lunch*

a.     Rice with stir-fry vegetables and 1 free-range skinless chicken breast.

b.     Mixed salad with bean shoots and 2-4 slices of dry wholemeal bread or rice cakes.

c.     Dried fruit with nuts and seeds followed by natural or soya yoghurt.

*Mid-Afternoon (3-4 p.m.)*

a.     3-5 pieces of fresh fruit (not bananas).

b.     2 or 3 rice cakes.

c.     1 slice of sprouted wheat loaf.

*Dinner*

a.      1 medium jacket potato with baked vegetables, chick peas and miso gravy or health store vegetable stock.

b.      Organic wholewheat pasta with vegetables and miso sauce.

c.      Rice, bean and vegetable stew.

d.      Boiled or poached egg with new potatoes and salad with bean shoots.

e.      Rice or other grain with fish and vegetables or a salad.

The above suggested menus are purely to give you some ideas. As long as you only eat foods from the RIGHT food list, you can make up you own menus. Also, you want to allow yourself enough room to be able to manage at least five meals per day. That's three main meals and two in between snacks. This is why you don't want to gorge yourself, so you can't eat for five or six hours. It is far better to pick little bits of the RIGHT foods all day if you want to speed up your metabolism and lose weight.

Don't eat too many bananas or avocados, they can be fattening at this stage. Try to eat at least one fresh salad every day and plenty of vegetables.

## Drinks

Drink plenty of water as often as you like. Bottled spring water, filtered or boiled, not straight from the tap. Don't drink carbonated bottled water, even if it is natural. It creates too much gas. Another habit that should be broken is drinking straight after a meal. This interferes with digestion and often causes gas and flatulence. Wait at least half an hour after eating before consuming liquids of any kind.

Water is important in the detoxification process, as it helps to carry away toxins. Do not limit your fluid intake. Drink!

Keep well away from all superstore squashes and so called fruit juice drinks.

All canned and bottled soft drinks, even low calorie ones are full of additives of all kinds. Don't touch them!

Coffee and tea is another potential problem. It may and most probably will interfere with the detoxification process as well as your efforts to improve liver function.

*(For other reasons to give up tea and coffee, refer to Chapter 1, page 10)*

Alcoholic drinks of all kinds should also be avoided. Mass brewing and rapidly produced forms of alcohol are part of a chemicalised industry. These chemicals, as well as pesticide residues, will undoubtedly be in these drinks. Good quality wines may be purchased and are likely to cause fewer problems to your liver than the cheaper ones. Organic wines are also available and these would be the wisest choice if you must drink at all.

Pressed juices are very good and can be purchased at most supermarkets. Health store organic pressed juices are by far the best for just a little extra money. Grape, apple and carrot juices are valuable for detoxification and may be drunk daily. Remember to always read the ingredient lists on all foods and drinks.

This chapter shows you what to eat as well as how much, under ideal conditions. I realise that you may not be able to always get or even afford organic or fresh vegetables. All you can hope to do is the best that you can. The thing to remember is, the closer you stick to the principles and guidelines outlined in this chapter, the healthier you will become and the slimmer you will be.

The amount you eat throughout the day is also a matter of individuality. As already mentioned, three main meals with two snacks in between, one at mid-morning and one at mid-afternoon is the target. Some of you will be laughing at this, as you already eat this much and more. However, some of you don't eat very much at all do you? Whatever your existing diet is, you must make adjustments accordingly to reach the above goal. It is true that having done this, some of you will naturally want to eat more at each meal than others. That is fine, providing the food you consume is from the RIGHT food category. For it is only when you start to eat these foods that you will begin to notice a significant decrease in your body size and an increase in your overall health.

# CHAPTER 9

## EXERCISE

*Warning:*

I advise everybody not to participate in any kind of rigorous physical activity, until the body has become accustomed to the diet plans outlined in Chapter 8. How long this takes depends on your discipline, lifestyle and individual requirements. Follow the week to week integration plan in Chapter 10 for the safest progress.

If correct exercise is a must for the physical body to keep it in good working order, it is especially important to a person undergoing a change of diet, whether to lose weight or for health reasons. It increases circulation (blood flow) and perspiration (sweat production). These two bodily functions help to release and eliminate toxins from within the body that have built up over many years, due to incorrect eating and failure to detoxify regularly. I must add here, that it would be possible to lose weight without moving a muscle. This weight could be shed through correct eating alone. Many people believe that all you need to do to lose weight is just begin to exercise more regularly. It is true that exercise burns calories, so theoretically speaking an increase in exercise would bring about a reduction in weight. However, this is not always the case. If you have ever tried to lose weight through exercise alone, you will have learned that it takes a lot of very hard work to lose a few pounds. This puts a lot of unnecessary stress upon many aspects of the body and in many cases could be quite dangerous. It is for this reason that diet and exercise must be carefully balanced to ensure the best and safest results.

## Correct Exercise

I consider the requirements of an individual's body to dictate what correct exercise is. By this I mean that everybody is different with their own personal needs. Choose an exercise that you enjoy. There are many to choose from. Maybe you don't think you will enjoy any. Then take a walk, but do something!

## How Often?

This is very important. You certainly do not want to overdo it. It is far better for you to be over cautious as far as exercise is concerned. This is especially true if you have never really exercised before. Even if you have exercised before, caution is of the utmost importance, as you never really know how the body is going to react. I have personally participated in many forms of exercise, including boxing, swimming, cycling, running (including two London marathons), Yoga, Tai Chi and martial arts. I first started running around my garden at about ten years old. Even now, after all this time, I am still careful if I haven't done anything for a little while. I allow my body time to adjust when starting a new training programme or recommencing an existing one after a lay-off.

# Rest

Just as important as starting slowly, is the need to rest between periods of increased activity. This allows your body time to recuperate. It is a fundamental aspect of any exercise routine or dietary change. Rest is essential for recovery and regeneration. When you sleep your body concentrates on repairing daytime wear and tear, as well as re-building long-term damage. Good rest and quality sleep is essential to your success. If anything is preventing you from getting a good night's sleep, then take action.

Bad habits can be changed. Too much tea or coffee in the evening can be over stimulating, so cut it out. If it is a case of noise, then invest in some comfortable ear plugs if the noise can't be stopped.

Your lifestyle may prevent you from getting enough rest. If you have children or a demanding husband, then you must grab your rest when you can. Speak to your husband about what you are trying to achieve. You have got to be a little selfish. Women can easily slip into the habit of living their lives for others. What about you? Of course, I'm not saying that you should neglect your family or your work, but it will certainly be very advantageous to you in many ways to get a break and some regular rest. This obviously applies to men too.

Stress is a big factor in western society and can lead to many emotional and physical problems. Try to reduce the stress in your life as best you can. Stress has the exact opposite effect on the human body compared to rest. Continual long-term stress can actually induce serious illnesses such as ulcers and heart disease.

Those of you who may be drawn to Tai Chi or Yoga, may want to consider following up on your interest here. These disciplines contain many aspects of relaxation through breathing exercises, meditation, visualisation and correct posture. Regular practice may help to reduce the stress in your life.

The liver needs as much oxygen as possible to help in detoxification and regeneration. Deep breathing exercises will help dramatically in this process. Your whole body, including your internal organs, will benefit from regular practice of these disciplines. Yoga and Tai Chi both contain many different breathing exercises.

Try to get proper instruction from a qualified teacher in the field of your choice. There are many classes available on these subjects nowadays, so it shouldn't be too difficult to find a class relatively close to your home. The Adult Education Board run many types of classes on all sorts of subjects. The relevant information for this can be found at your local library. Books on these subjects may also be found.

The required amount of rest and sleep is very important early on as your body will be going through many changes due to the new eating routines from the previous chapter. The required amount of rest and sleep means as much as you need. Ignore other people's standards! Listen to your body. Rest or sleep whenever you feel like it, or at least whenever you can.

So it is correct eating, the right amount of exercise and ample rest cleverly combined, that will ensure a safe and permanent reduction in weight. This will in time produce a stronger, healthier body. A slimmer one too!

## Getting Started

As you can appreciate, it is impossible for me to know exactly what you need as far as exercise is concerned, or anything else for that matter. All I can do through a book is to give you guidelines. You will have to judge for yourself how you feel at any one given time and use the guidelines wisely and to your advantage. You will not get it right all the time, you are bound to make mistakes. This is how we learn. That is why you must start to exercise slowly, to allow yourself time to adjust. In this way the mistakes won't be too costly. On the other hand, if you are over zealous, you may find yourself exhausted. This will not only hinder your progress but could be detrimental to your health, as well as frustrating if you have things to do and don't have the energy to do them. Be wise and start slowly with anything new, especially exercise.

# First Steps

Invest in a new pair of training shoes if you don't already have some. Also a tracksuit is a good idea. These items are not only good for exercise, but get you in the mood a little and help to make you feel good about what you are doing. It's worth spending a little extra money to get a good pair of trainers if you can afford to. Comfort makes training all the more easier. Equally as important, is getting the right type of footwear for your choice of activity, be it running, squash, tennis aerobics or any other activity. Some trainers can be used for a variety of sports. However, if you are going to stick to one activity religiously, it is worth purchasing the correct type of footwear. This is because different sports place different stresses on your body. Wearing the correct footwear supports your feet and ankles where they need to be supported, as they are specifically designed for this purpose. This will reduce unnecessary stresses on your body.

Having said all of this, don't go spending a fortune on the top of the range sports shoes at this stage. Many of you will probably have done very little training of any kind if any at all, so you will be starting your exercise routine with walking or light aerobics. The need for expensive trainers therefore, is not really necessary. However, if you have plenty of money to invest in nice training equipment, then why not! As already mentioned, comfort and the right type of shoe makes your exercise more enjoyable. Safer too!

In order for you to start exercising correctly, there are five main points for you to consider. They are:

1.    Your size

2.    How active you are now

3.    Your experience with exercise

4.    Your age

5.    Do you have any disabilities/health conditions?

## Your Size

Your size will obviously have an effect on the type of activity you will be able to do. I once read somewhere of a man that hadn't been outside of his house for many years due to his massive size. This would have dictated what type of exercise he was able to do. Not because he couldn't get outside to exercise, but rather due to his massive size preventing him from being agile enough to participate in that exercise. This type of person would find it very difficult just to walk a short distance. Therefore, he would concentrate on the diet and forget about exercise until he had lost enough weight to increase his walking distance. For a forty stone individual this may take anything from one to six months, depending on the person. Patience and willpower are required here, as mentioned in previous chapters.

Once he had lost enough weight to be able to walk more easily, he would increase the distance a little more or decrease the distance and increase the speed. Alternatively, he may keep the distance the same and increase the speed. Just walking around the garden a few times is enough for some people. You must judge for yourself where you are and start training at a pace you think is suitable for you. Just remember to START SLOWLY for reasons already discussed.

## How active you are

Perhaps you already participate in some form of exercise. Maybe you are a busy person due to your work. That is physically busy, not mentally busy. You can be busy all day sitting down. This is not physically active and doesn't constitute exercise. However, if you are on your feet 4-7 hours a day, 4-7 days a week and you are relatively active during these periods, this is a different matter. If this is you, you can start by a walk around the block once or twice a week. Take into consideration that 10-15 minutes would be once around the block. As already said, start slowly and see how your body reacts before increasing to a light jog. 10-15 minutes on a cycling machine is another option and may be adopted in place of a walk or a jog.

If you are physically very active during the day, you may find that you are too tired for exercise. If this is the case, then listen to your body and rest. Exercise only when you feel strong enough to do so. This will be dealt with in the following chapter.

## Experience

If you have participated in sports activity before, then you will be quite familiar with exercising and hopefully won't find it a problem to get motivated. You will also have some idea of the effects exercising has on your body. It doesn't matter how experienced you are, if you haven't done anything for a while, always START SLOWLY. In this way you won't experience too many unpleasant side effects like aching muscles, a tight chest and/or fatigue.

## Your Age

Your age is obviously a predominating factor in the type of exercise you will be able to do. It will have an even bigger effect on the level at which you will be able to achieve. However, it is never too late to take up exercise. Once again, START SLOWLY and BUILD UP GRADUALLY. I think, when you are in your later years, it is far more beneficial for you to participate in the types of exercise that have a less negative effect on your body. Light stretching, swimming, cycling, walking and Tai Chi. Most of these exercises increase circulation, improve flexibility and exercise the heart and lungs without putting too much strain on the joints.

## Tai Chi

Tai Chi doesn't work the heart and lungs like the other more aerobic exercises do, but the emphasis on posture and correct breathing, energises the whole body. The principles and regular practice of Tai Chi, increase bodily awareness and internal health tenfold. It's a wonderful exercise for the elderly, as it is graceful and gentle in its approach, unlike that of the more physically demanding aerobic activities.

Tai Chi isn't only good for the elderly though. It's never too early to learn about your body. If we were all taught the correct way to stand, walk, sit and move from an early age, there would be fewer physical problems in the world today. Tai Chi teaches us these things.

## Disabilities

If you have a disability, then it is something you will obviously need to consider. A change of diet doesn't pose any problems. However, exercise might. You know more about your disability if you have one than I do, so you will have a better understanding of its nature and what type of exercise suits it best. Having said this, Tai Chi and swimming spring to mind as they are both gentle in their approach. The point to remember is, don't let your disability stop you from exercising. Even if you can only exercise one half of your body, or one limb, it must be better than not exercising at all.

There is a man who I have seen walking around my father's area many times. Each time I see him, he is miles away from the places I have seen him before. He is therefore walking great distances regularly. This man has a severe disability as he has an extremely bad limp and he holds one arm and shoulder in an awkward manner. It looks like he may have suffered from polio or a bad accident. The point is, that walking is clearly difficult for him and I would imagine that he is in some discomfort or pain. Yet he doesn't give up. He marches on, literally. He covers many miles and has been doing so over a number of years. Perhaps we should all try to learn from such a shining example of courage, strength and determination. Maybe you are like this man yourself. Then I take my hat off to you too.

## Health Conditions

High blood pressure or asthma can pose some serious problems for certain individuals wishing to start an exercise routine, as can angina and other heart related diseases. Once again, I must stress START SLOWLY and BUILD UP GRADUALLY. The chances are if you are excessively overweight you will be suffering from at least one of the above conditions. Over time these conditions and others may greatly improve through correct eating, combined with gentle to moderate exercise.

Many people would consider that to be overweight is a disability in itself. I would be inclined to agree. Being grossly overweight would stop you from doing many things. In extreme cases just moving around would be (and is for some people) very difficult.

A good idea would be to join a sports centre. These places have professional equipment and qualified staff who are well educated in physical exercise, whether you have a disability, health problem, weight condition or just want to get fit. Talk to the fitness instructor there about what you want to achieve and any concerns you might have. They should be able to assess you and give you a proper training programme that is structured especially for your individual needs.

If you don't feel happy with the instructor for any reason and are not confident about training without instruction, you must find somebody else to guide you. It is very important to feel right about what you are doing. You don't want any negative thoughts or feelings as they will only hamper your progress.

The Yellow Pages is a good place to look and you should have no trouble finding a sports centre or health and fitness club in your area.

However, for those of you who prefer to do things alone, the next chapter shows you how to combine diet, exercise and rest, into a week to week integrated plan.

# CHAPTER 10

# WEEK TO WEEK INTEGRATION PLAN

*Warning:*

If you are in any doubt whatsoever about your physical condition and the effects exercise or a change of diet may have on you, consult your GP or other medical professional. This is especially so if you are pregnant, lactating, elderly or have a serious health problem.

This chapter is for guidance only, as each of you are individuals. It combines all the previous chapters into an integrated whole, to guide you to a safe and permanent reduction in weight. It is designed for an average individual and you will not be that person, as one does not exist. Therefore, how long each stage takes, depends upon your own physical, emotional and psychological needs. You will learn from this book and experience gained from continual self-evaluation, when to move on to the next stage from any given point in this chapter.

You should try to think positively about your weight loss. Don't think of it as a burden and a chore that you have to do. Instead, try to think of it as an exciting, interesting and learnful journey to a new way of being. YOU CAN DO IT!

**Week 1**

Objectives:   Self-evaluation

Tasks:        Acknowledge pollutants in your life
              Environmental and dietary

This first week is mainly preparation. Start looking at yourself and your lifestyle to find out what might contribute to your condition. How many foods do you consume from the WRONG food list? How much food do you consume? Are you unhappy? Are you depressed? Why? Take notes if you feel the need. Be honest about yourself and at the same time try to keep your self-esteem up. Look for your good points also and remind yourself of what you WILL achieve. Read Chapter 2 again – Reasons for Losing Weight.

*POLLUTANTS*

Begin to acknowledge the environmental pollutants in your life. What are the major sources? This applies to both work and home. Think about what ones you can do without the most. Read Chapter 4 – Detoxification, again if need be.

If you are a smoker, take note of how many cigarettes you consume and under what conditions you consume the most. Social, stress etc.

*DIET*

Pollutants in your food, as by now you must know, are a big problem. Read all the ingredient lists on everything you consume. Purchase a book on 'E' numbers or food additives. This will give you some idea of what you are doing to your body and help to motivate you to give these foods up for good. Then you will be slim for good too!

## EXERCISE

You will not be doing any real exercise at this stage. Rather, just start to think of ways that you can bring exercise into your daily life. Do you live, or work close to a swimming baths or leisure centre? Could you walk or cycle to work, etc?

## REST

Assess and recognise any barriers between you and good rest/sleep. This might be a time to look at how many cups of tea or coffee you consume each day. Sugar, as well as caffeine, is a big factor here, as they are both stimulating to the system.

What else keeps you from having a good night's sleep? Do you like to sit up watching television? Do you feel like you are not living if you go to bed early? These are issues you need to look at if you want to get quality sleep. Quality sleep is essential for reasons previously discussed.

If you dream a lot and wake up feeling like you haven't slept, it will more than likely be due to the many additives in your diet. This is especially so with confectionery, as the many additives and high levels of sugar they contain are extremely stimulating to the system.

## SELF-ACKNOWLEDGEMENT

Applaud yourself at the information you have gathered and the fact that you have acknowledged much of your problem. When we acknowledge things, we can begin to change them. You are another step closer to being and looking like you want to. Feel good about it and give yourself a pat on the back.

## Week 2

Objectives:  Remove Pollutants

Tasks:  Find a good health store

## POLLUTANTS

Make changes in your home by discarding air pollutants such as air fresheners, insect killers and other aerosol sprays.

Smokers should start to think about reducing their intake. Be realistic, don't try to give up completely.

## DIET

Find a good health store and start to buy basic foods or what you fancy from the RIGHT food list. Begin to discontinue with high additive foods, particularly dairy, flour products and confectionery as from the WRONG food list. Don't cut these foods out completely, just reduce your intake by 20-40%. Fill the gap with the RIGHT foods. If you are the type of person that doesn't really eat that much at all, then increase your intake from the RIGHT food list, remembering to eat little and often.  Aim for three meals a day at this stage.

Take another look at your tea and coffee consumption and start to think about alternatives from the health store.  Substitute one of your existing beverages for one of these alternatives every day of this week.  Step up your water intake as well.  Two or three full glasses to be drunk every day.

Visit your local library or purchase a cookbook suitable for the type of diet you will be eating.  Macrobiotics, cooking for health, or something similar.  This might help you in the early stages to make this plainer food seem a little more interesting and make the transition a little easier.  Good health stores often stock these types of books.

*EXERCISE*

*Breathing*

Most people, young and old, breathe by raising and opening the chest cavity.  Many athletes and sports people breathe in this way as well.  This is how our breathing has developed over the years, from early childhood.  This type of breathing only utilises a third of the lungs, thus depriving your system of vital oxygen.

The aim of the following breathing exercise is to return to the powerful, deep abdominal breathing we were born with.  If it is practised regularly, it will become part of your natural breathing pattern.  This will aid in detoxification and help to energise your whole body, as well as giving a gentle massage to your internal organs. It can be practised standing or sitting.

*Standing*

Stand with your feet a shoulder width apart. Do not lean back or forward. Try to keep your body in a straight line, using a side view mirror if you have to. Try to stand so your weight is evenly distributed over your feet. You don't want to be back on your heels or up on your toes. Allow your legs to bend a little, drop your shoulders and gently relax the chest by allowing it to sink inward slightly. Place one hand on your navel or just below, and the other hand on top of that hand. If this is difficult due to your size, then just allow your arms to hang naturally by your side. Close your eyes and focus your attention on your abdomen. Relax. Gently and slowly breathe in through your nose, allowing your abdomen to naturally fill up under your hand. Do not force your belly outward. It is your breathing that allows your abdomen to move in this way, nothing else. It must happen naturally. Quietly and slowly breathe out through the nose. As you exhale, consciously draw your abdomen in so it feels as though you are squeezing the air out of your torso from the bottom up. Exhale fully, until you feel that you have emptied your lungs.

Aim for a count of three or four on the in breath and the same for the out breath. Try to stay relaxed throughout, keeping your breathing deep, slow and even.

*Sitting*

The technique for this is exactly the same as when standing. Once again, keep your feet a shoulder width apart, or slightly wider, your spine upright and allow your shoulders to round slightly forward, gently relaxing the chest. Breathe deep and slow into your abdomen for a count of three or four for one inhalation and the same for the exhalation. Remember to stay mentally and physically relaxed throughout. This will take practice.

The count of three or four for the inhalation and exhalation is purely a guideline to create a deep, slow rhythmic breathing pattern. It must not be forced in any way. Try to breathe naturally with emphasis on your abdomen. Of course, conscious effort is required, but not force.

Practise the above deep breathing exercise (sitting or standing) for five minutes, twice a day. If you practise close to bedtime it may relax you and help to give you a good night's sleep. On the other hand, it may energise you and wake you up! If you find it too energising near bedtime, then don't practise after 6 p.m. You will learn what is best for you and make changes accordingly.

*REST*

If you are still having problems sleeping properly of a night-time, it needs to be addressed. Look at what you are eating or drinking. If you are eating high additive food after 6 p.m., then this needs to be changed.  Coffee or tea also shouldn't be consumed after this time.  Don't forget, use your ear plugs and a travel mask if your sleeping is disrupted due to noise or light, and try to get an afternoon nap if you can, or just rest generally whenever you get the chance.

Try to look once again at the stress factors in your life and do your best to minimise them.  This may be the time to start looking for Tai Chi or Yoga classes.

## Week 3

Objectives:    Begin detoxification

Tasks:             Remove pollutants

*POLLUTANTS*

Continue to remove any pollutants from your home or at least discontinue using them. Smokers, continue to cut down on your intake.  You may want to eat more as a result of your decrease in cigarette consumption. Great!  From the RIGHT food category though.

*DIET*

Continue to substitute high additive foods for those from the RIGHT food category. Aim for a reduction of your previous intake of WRONG foods, to around 40-60%.  That means eating roughly half the quantity of WRONG foods that you used to eat.  Eat RIGHT foods in their place.  Have a look at some healthy alternatives to confectionery (chocolate bars etc.) if you must eat this type of food.  Just remember, if you want to lose weight and keep it off, these foods may only be eaten in moderation and not very often. Don't forget to read the ingredient lists on everything that you consume.

Try to substitute two of your normal daytime drinks such as tea or coffee, for healthier alternatives from the RIGHT food category. What you put in your drinks, healthy or not, should be changing by now also. Those of you who already consume semi-skimmed milk, should now start the transition over to fully skimmed. Full fat milk drinkers should start moving over to semi-skimmed.

Sugar should also be reduced now by at least 50%. That means cutting your intake by half. Also, the sugar that you continue to use should be of a healthier variety. Dark brown forms such as demerara and muscovado are the least refined and should be used for this reason. They are sometimes described as raw cane sugar.

*EXERCISE*

Continue with your daily practice of deep breathing. Buy yourself a new pair of trainers if you can afford to and a tracksuit. Though just a sweatshirt and a pair of jogging bottoms will do. Start to take a walk every couple of days if you don't lead a very active life, with your work etc. If you are quite active, then just carry on as you are for now. For the walkers, just a walk for 15 minutes or so will suffice.

## REST

Continue to make sure you are getting enough sleep and rest. Early nights are important. If you can't get to sleep, then try a cup of camomile tea before you retire (health store). Stick with it and eventually your body will start to become accustomed to the earlier bedtime.

You shouldn't be experiencing any real side effects from the detoxification process, as we are going at a relatively slow speed. A slight headache maybe at most, although I doubt it. Acne also is another common symptom. You can't expect to eat so many WRONG foods for so long and not have to pay a price of some kind when you start to detoxify. Drink plenty of water and the symptoms will pass, but remember, if you do get a slight headache you must try not to go pouring more toxins into your bloodstream again in the form of painkillers. This would be contrary to what we are trying to achieve here.

## MEDICATION

For those of you that use medication, now is the time to seek other alternatives. I speak here mainly of the flippant pill users that take tablets for any occasion. A slight headache, a stomach upset, or insomnia to name but a few. Not of the man or woman that takes medication for more serious conditions such as angina, asthma or diabetes. However, even these conditions may be helped with herbalism or homeopathy. Speak to your doctor about phasing out your medication, though not many western doctors warm to the idea of herbalism or homeopathy. If you don't like the response from your GP, then seek alternative advice. Addresses and phone numbers can be found at the back of this book for relevant organisations.

## Week 4

Objectives:    Detoxification

Tasks:           Remove Pollutants

*POLLUTANTS*

All environmental pollution should now be removed from your home and as much as possible from your workplace. Smokers really should be cutting back on your consumption now. Aim for at least a third less in the amount of cigarettes you consume. Don't forget about ways that might help you – acupuncture, anti-smoking clinics etc.

*DIET*

For this week, aim for a reduction of 60-80% of WRONG foods and an increase of foods from the RIGHT food group. In simple terms, this will mean that just over half to roughly three quarters of your diet will consist of RIGHT foods. Also, you need to be eating little and often. Aim for five small meals a day or three main meals, with light snacks in between. If you are struggling to do this, then eat less at each sitting.

Tea and coffee consumption should also continue to decline. At least three quarters of your original intake of these types of drinks should now start to be replaced with natural fruit juices (preferably pressed), vegetable juices, herb teas, dandelion root coffee and spring or filtered water. If you don't have a water filter, then now is the time to buy one.

Those of you who want to sprout your own shoots should be starting this now. It is worth the effort as they provide the body with essential nutrients.

Alcohol should also be reduced to a minimum if you want to lose weight. A drop of wine here and there is ok but don't drink too much. It's bad for the liver and will hinder the detoxification process.

*EXERCISE*

Increase your daily practice of deep breathing to three times a day. This can be done anywhere. Sitting on a train, on your work chair or a park bench. Though not when driving, for obvious reasons. Alternatively, stick to twice a day and increase the time to ten minutes for each sitting.

Continue with your walks but step up the pace slightly for a fifteen minute time span. If you have a dog and already walk, but find that the time you are out is longer than fifteen minutes, then break it up with one or two periods of increased activity for a few minutes each time. Walking faster for a few minutes here and there whilst you are out with your dog, will get you fitter and slimmer, when combined with correct eating habits.

This principle can be applied to all types of exercise and if you are cycling to work or walking, it can be adopted here also.

If you have a cycling machine, then the same applies. Fifteen minutes, alternating slightly with increased periods of activity (cycling faster for short periods).

A good method is a combination of increased activity and increased endurance. By this I mean, on Monday take your fifteen minute walk at a slightly increased rate and on Wednesday increase the distance to say thirty minutes. However, on the thirty minute walk, adopt the original pace that you first started with when walking for fifteen minutes for the first time. Having a day off in between gives your body time to recuperate.

Combine these methods for this week and remember to monitor yourself as you go. That is, during your exercise and afterwards also.

*REST*

Ensure you are getting plenty of quality sleep. Rest whenever you can to maximise healing.

*SELF-ACKNOWLEDGEMENT*

If you have reached this stage, although it is still early on, applaud yourself. If you are finding it difficult, remind yourself of your objectives and push on. DON'T'GIVE UP.

## Weeks 5 and 6

Objectives:    Detoxification/Liver regeneration

Tasks:          Increase physical activity

*POLLUTANTS*

The only environmental pollutant that should be left at this stage is smoking. If you are a smoker, you ought to be smoking only half the amount of cigarettes that you were smoking before week 1 of this chapter. If you aren't, then you need to try and achieve this goal before the end of week 6. If you can't then read the section on cigarettes again in Chapter 4 – Detoxification and just keep trying. Try to set yourself a realistic target when to give up smoking completely.

*DIET*

By the end of week 6, try to decrease your WRONG food intake by 70-90%. That means your RIGHT food consumption will have increased to just under three quarters, to nearly all of what you eat. Aim for the five small meals a day, or three main ones, with snacks in between, depending on your appetite.

Try to phase out tea and coffee by the end of the sixth week if you can. However, if a cup of tea or coffee keeps you sane at this stage, then that is fine. You don't want to be unhappy or miserable, so allowances can and ought to be made. Drink plenty of water.

## EXERCISE

Slowly begin to increase the intensity of your walks or whatever exercise you have chosen. Aim for a fifteen minute walk at a steady, brisk pace and see how you feel. If it seems too difficult, then slow down when you need to and build up again. Keep an eye on your posture, making sure you are walking upright with your head up and your shoulders relaxed. Don't forget to breathe, preferably deeply for maximum oxygen intake and absorption. There's a lot more in walking than meets the eye! Take a longer walk once a week to build up stamina and keep with the one day on and one day off routine for now.

## REST

Continue to get early nights and rest whenever you can. If your lifestyle is proving too difficult for you to relax, then find a Tai Chi or Yoga teacher and learn some deep relaxation techniques. Alternatively, change your lifestyle.

## Weeks 7 and 8

Objectives:    Detoxification/Liver regeneration

Tasks:         Increase physical activity

## POLLUTANTS

Smokers, continue to cut down on your consumption if you haven't given up yet. Smoking will certainly hold you back when trying to increase your exercise intensity. Kick the habit and fill the gap with food from the RIGHT food group.

*DIET*

Try to aim for 90% of what you eat to be from the RIGHT food group, by the end of the eighth week. That's close to a diet consisting exclusively of these foods. If you experience any detoxification symptoms such as fatigue, depression, or headaches, then rest and drink herbal teas or fruit juices and these symptoms should pass. If they don't and you are concerned, you should resume some of your old eating habits, as it is a sign that you may be detoxifying too quickly. However, don't overdo it or you will find you will be back where you started in a matter of days. Don't use this as an excuse to undo all the good work you have achieved up until now. Stay in control and keep focused on the slimmer you.

*EXERCISE*

Carry on with your walks as with weeks 5 & 6. If you are comfortable with your exercise and don't experience any real discomfort or unpleasantness, either during your exercise, or on your day off, increase your routine to two days on and one day off.

## Example:

*Monday:*      15-20 minutes brisk walking

*Tuesday:*     20-30 minutes steady walking

*Wednesday:* Rest

| | |
|---|---|
| *Thursday:* | 30 minutes steady walking, with short periods (1-2 minutes) of increased activity every 10 minutes |
| *Friday:* | 15-20 minutes brisk walking |
| *Saturday:* | Rest |
| *Sunday:* | Repeat, treating this day as Monday and so on. Alternatively, if you are feeling tired, rest on this day and start from Monday as before. Or you could take a gentle walk before commencing on Monday again |

If you have sore feet or ankles due to new trainers and the new mileage, change your activity to swimming or cycling. In fact, this is a good idea anyway, as it adds variation for both your mind and your body. Try changing one or two days a week to a different type of exercise and see how you feel. Just remember to always start slow when trying something for the first time.

*REST*

Early nights and quality sleep a must. Continue to rest whenever you get the chance

## Weeks 9-12

| | |
|---|---|
| Objectives: | Detoxification/Liver regeneration |
| Tasks: | Increase physical activity |

## POLLUTANTS

Smokers, set yourself a date to give up and do it!

## DIET

If you want to lose weight significantly, you need to be eating a 100% RIGHT food diet. That means no WRONG foods whatsoever. Give up tea and coffee completely and drink natural fruit and vegetable juices in their place. Herb teas and cereal drinks may also be drunk. However, only skimmed milk should be used now and sugar needs to be at an absolute minimum if you are to secure that weight loss. Three teaspoonfuls a day maximum is ok at this stage, but quite honestly sugar is best left out of the diet. Try honey in its place. This is a much healthier alternative, but once again don't overdo it. Three to four teaspoonfuls a day maximum can be used.

Remember to make sure you are eating plenty of foods from the tables on pages 48 and 49. Foods rich in iron, folic acid and vitamin C respectfully.

Drinkers – give up alcohol completely, it's bad for your liver and it's undoing all the hard work you have put in.

Drink plenty of water, making sure you are consuming at least two pints during the course of the day. If this is a struggle, then drink as much as you feel comfortable with. Just make sure you don't get too thirsty. A steady flow of juices and water throughout the day, will help to carry the toxins away!

*EXERCISE*

As you begin to feel more comfortable with your exercise routines, start to build up to daily training with one day off a week. Keep the intensity the same as for weeks 7 and 8, but add an extra day's training from week 9 onwards. If you are following the example for an exercise schedule from weeks 7 and 8, it will mean that you will now start training on Wednesday or Saturday as well. Once again, when you are comfortable with this, add the other day, say at week 10 or 11 for example. You will then be exercising six days a week with Sunday off.

**Example:**

Week 9

*Monday:*     15-20 minutes brisk walking

*Tuesday:*     20-30 minutes steady walking

*Wednesday:* Rest

*Thursday:*     30 minutes steady walking or cycling with short periods of increased activity

*Friday:*     20-30 minutes of steady walking or cycling machine

*Saturday:*     15-20 minutes brisk walking

*Sunday:*     Rest

**Example:**

Weeks 10 or 11-12

*Monday:*      15-20 minutes brisk walking

*Tuesday:*     20-30 minutes steady walking

*Wednesday:* 30 minutes of steady walking or cycling
with short periods of increased activity

*Thursday:*    20-30 minutes steady walking, cycling or
swimming

*Friday:*        15-20 minutes of brisk walking or cycling

*Saturday:*     30 minutes of steady walking or cycling
with short periods of increased activity

*Sunday:*      Rest

The above examples are for guidance only. As already mentioned, DO NOT MOVE ON TO ANY STAGE UNTIL YOU FEEL COMFORTABLE WITH THE PRECEDING ONE. Be patient, build up gradually and you will be fine.

If you have any injuries of any kind, change your exercise to take the pressure away from that area. If all types of exercise aggravate it, then rest until it has healed. Commence exercising at a stage below the one you were on when the injury occurred and build up gradually again.

*REST*

Early nights and quality sleep are essential. Try to stay as relaxed and calm as possible, as much as possible, even in potentially stressful situations. Easier said than done I know, but try - it's good for the liver. Rest during the day whenever you get the chance.

If you have reached this stage, you should give yourself a big pat on the back. Even if it has taken you longer than twelve weeks, it is still a big achievement. Feel good about yourself and push on to greater heights.

**Weeks 13-18**

Objectives:    Detoxification/Liver regeneration

Tasks:         Metabolise fat

ATTENTION:

This section of the plan should only be started if you have carefully gone through all of the previous stages. It doesn't matter if you have taken longer to get to this stage. In fact, that would probably be better, as it is more beneficial to do it slowly and correctly than to be in a rush and miss out important aspects of what we are trying to achieve.

If you are not sure or comfortable with this or any other part of the plan, then stick with a level that suits your needs. You can burn your fat off slowly and just as permanently with long walks, providing you continue to eat mainly from the RIGHT food group and stay away from WRONG foods.

*POLLUTANTS*

Smokers give up! Get help if you can't. Keep trying.

*DIET*

Continue to eat only RIGHT foods, not forgetting those from the tables on pages 48 and 49. You may want to increase your carbohydrate intake to compensate for the increased activity that is to follow. Baked potatoes, rice, pasta and bread respectively, may be eaten in slightly larger quantities if need be. Though don't overdo it. You should be eating three main meals per day, plus snacks in between. If you are not hungry, but not stuffed, you should be getting all the nutrients and carbohydrates you need. If you feel hungry, then eat. If you still feel hungry, then increase your carbohydrate intake, but not too much to kill your appetite for too long.

Drink plenty of water, two or three hours before any rigorous training session and plenty afterwards too. I've found pressed green grape juice to be a wonderful revitaliser after a hard training session, due to its natural fruit sugar content. This can be purchased from most supermarkets.

*EXERCISE*

This is the part of the plan where we start to increase the exercise intensity, to break down that fat. This would have happened to some extent already, as you should have already noticed a difference to the shape of your body in the mirror.

Make sure you are completely comfortable with the previous exercise programme (weeks 9-12) before continuing any further.

For the first two weeks of this period (weeks 13 and 14) start to increase your walks to a gentle jog. By this stage, it shouldn't be too difficult initially, but you may suffer a little the day after. For this reason you are going to go back to the one day on, one day off routine. Jogging one day and walking or some other lighter exercise the next and so on.

## Example:

Weeks 13 and 14

*Monday:* 15-20 minutes light jogging

*Tuesday:* 20-30 minutes of steady walking or gentle cycling

*Wednesday:* 20 minutes of light jogging

*Thursday:* 20-30 minutes of walking, swimming, cycling or skipping. Alternatively, you can rest on this day if you need to.

| Friday: | 20 minutes light jogging |
| Saturday: | 20-30 minutes of walking or gentle cycling |
| Sunday: | Rest |

For the next two weeks of this period, (weeks 15 and 16), start to increase the intensity of your jogging. Only do this if you are comfortable with the previous two weeks. Also, whenever you start a training session, do it slowly. Start off at a slow pace, to allow your body time to warm up thoroughly before increasing the intensity. Hold yourself back slightly, even if you feel good when training and wait to see how you feel the next day. This way you can be sure of not overdoing it. Apply this principle always, no matter how fit you are.

**Example:**

Weeks 15 and 16

| Monday: | 15-20 minutes of light to moderate jogging |
| Tuesday: | 20-30 minutes of steady walking or gentle cycling |
| Wednesday: | 20 minutes of light to moderate jogging. |
| Thursday: | 20-30 minutes of walking, swimming or other exercise. Alternatively, rest if need be |

| *Friday:* | 20 minutes of light to moderate jogging |
|---|---|
| *Saturday:* | 20-30 minutes of walking or gentle cycling |
| *Sunday:* | Rest |

For the last two weeks of this period (weeks 17 and 18), increase the intensity of your jogging further. Once again, only if you feel comfortable to do so. Because of the increased activity on your jogging days and the extra stress on your body for these two weeks, your non-jogging days will become less active. This gives your body a well-earned rest and time to repair.

**Example:**

Weeks 17 and 18

| *Monday:* | 15-20 minutes of light to moderate to brisk running |
|---|---|
| *Tuesday:* | 5-10 minutes on the cycling machine and a light stretch |
| *Wednesday:* | 20-30 minutes of moderate to brisk running |
| *Thursday:* | A 10 minute walk, followed by light stretching |
| *Friday:* | 10-15 minutes of gentle to moderate cycling, followed by a 20 minute moderate to brisk run |

*Saturday:*    A 10 minute walk, followed by light stretching

*Sunday:*    Rest

In order to metabolise your fat and lose weight through exercising, you need to do enough to finish your training session tired and soaked in sweat. Though be careful not to do too much. If you wake up the following morning after a training session with a headache or you feel nauseous, exhausted or generally debilitated, it is a sure sign that you have overdone it. Rest and take it easier next time.

Once again, never train on an injury. There really is no point in injuring yourself, even to lose weight, no matter how determined you are. You need to be clever as well as courageous. If you have an injury, keep active in other ways while resting it.

If you feel ill at any time for any reason, decrease your activity levels, or stop altogether until it has passed. Recommence training when you are able to do so, at a lower level and build up again from there.

*REST*

Early nights and quality sleep is as important as ever. Rest and relax properly after every training session.

**Weeks 19-25**

Objectives:    Strengthen liver capacity

Tasks:    Metabolise fat through increased activity

## DIET

Continue as before, eating only foods from the RIGHT food group. For this period though, eat your last meal of the day three hours before your training session. This obviously applies to training days only. For example, eat your last meal at 6 p.m. and take a run at 9 p.m. Don't eat anything else at all, until mid-morning the following day, say at 10 a.m. However, drink as much water, diluted fruit juices or herb teas as you like.

When this type of eating pattern is combined with the appropriate exercise, the liver's glycogen stores are run down, thereby maximising fat reduction and weight loss. To understand this fully, we need to go into a little more detail.

Glucose is a simple form of sugar carried in the bloodstream. It is used directly by the body for energy. Few foods other than grapes, contain pure glucose. Therefore, the body obtains most of its glucose from the breaking down of starches during digestion.

When the body absorbs more glucose than it needs to meet immediate energy demands, it stores the excess in the liver and muscles. These glucose units linked together are called glycogen. This glycogen is your energy reserve. It can be broken down and quickly released back into the bloodstream when needed, such as during exercise.

By not exercising for three hours since your last meal, you can be certain that by the time you do exercise, that last meal would have been converted into glycogen. The idea is, if you exercise for long enough, you will use up your body's glycogen stores, from both the liver and the muscles (although it is the liver that we are concerned with here). The liver then recharges itself with glycogen for future energy requirements. This would normally be from food, as you would usually eat again relatively soon after exercising. However, you aren't going to eat again until the following morning. This means that the liver is forced to recharge from other sources. The most available source is excess adipose tissue, more commonly known as fat. Basically, your liver will be drawing from your body fat to recharge itself with glycogen. In a nutshell, you will be losing weight while you are asleep. It's as simple as that!

On the less active days, you can eat in the evening if you are hungry, though always allow at least two hours to lapse after eating before you retire. Don't eat too late!

*EXERCISE*

You need to exercise long and hard enough to run down the liver's glycogen stores, so it can recharge itself with your body fat during the night. Thirty to forty five minutes of continuous, moderate exercise should do it. Don't forget to wait three hours after the last meal of the day before you start. Practice this routine every other day of this time period, providing you feel strong enough to do so.

**Example:**

Weeks 19-25

*Monday:* 30-45 minutes of steady to moderate running. Light stretching afterwards

*Tuesday:* Some gentle cycling, a walk or other activity. Go with how you feel

*Wednesday:* 30-45 minutes on the cycling machine or a run of the same duration

*Thursday:* The same as Tuesday

*Friday:* 30-45 minutes of circuit training (be careful) i.e. press-ups, sit-ups, squat thrusts, star jumps etc. Alternatively, 20 minutes of cycling or skipping, followed by a 20 minute run. Light stretching afterwards

*Saturday:* As Tuesday

*Sunday:* Rest

*REST*

After your training sessions, take a shower and go straight to bed. Continue with your early nights as often as possible and rest as usual during the day.

## Week 26 onwards

*DIET*

By this stage, I would imagine that you have got a pretty good idea about how your body reacts to different types of food. I say this because most of you would have gone backwards and forwards with the diet change. Very few people would have stuck to their guns from the word go. I know I have found it difficult myself, so I know how hard it is.

Continue with your diet of RIGHT foods, but reduce the amount of meals you eat during the day to two or three. So basically you will be cutting out the snacks in between. Go with how you feel on this though, as the most important aspect is to eat only RIGHT foods and to keep active. If you really feel hungry, then you should eat. Don't overdo it though. Keep with the principles of little and often.

If you do go off the rails a little as far as your diet is concerned, try to stay in control of it. I know this is difficult if you are the type of person who loves your food, but don't get caught in the trap of obsessive eating. Try to be aware of yourself and if you are going to over eat, try to stick to the RIGHT foods as much as possible.

## EXERCISE

Try to keep as active as you can. A good training session every other day or even three times a week, is a good thing. You know how your body reacts to different types of exercise by now, so use this experience to keep active and to keep learning. Try new activities, such as squash, tennis, netball, indoor or outdoor mountain climbing and even golf. You cover a good two or three miles when walking around a golf course. Great exercise!

Although, as I have previously stated, I am not a lover of too many tablets etc. A nutritional supplement such as a slow release multi-vitamin and mineral, is not a bad idea. This is especially so if you are very active. However, I still maintain that if you are eating enough of a healthy balanced diet, you will be getting everything you need. It's up to you. If you do decide to take a supplement, make sure you buy the best one. The cheaper ones usually have a lot of binders and fillers that are not always easily digestible. You get what you pay for, as with everything.

Visit your local library and take a look at some of the many books they have on sport. You might get some new ideas on training techniques or different activities that you might like to pursue. Start to read health and fitness magazines to add to your knowledge of diet and exercise.

# CHAPTER 11

## STAYING SLIM

For many of you, this will be the most difficult part of your journey. Once the initial excitement and enthusiasm of starting something new has worn off, you'll have to contend with the boring, monotonous, continuation of the meal plans outlined in this book. At least, that is how many of you will see it. For those of you who do feel this way, try to be a little more positive in your thoughts and feelings.

You may have found that you have gone back to your old eating habits. Maybe this is a reflection that you rushed in too quickly. Sometimes over-enthusiasm has a way of making us fall flat on our faces. This usually brings disappointment and a feeling of failure. You need to slow down but don't give up. Take yourself back to the beginning of the previous chapter and start again at a pace that suits *you*. Allow yourself time to change at a slower rate. It can take years to change habits of a lifetime, so be patient but just keep trying.

Having worked through this book and especially the last chapter, you will have learnt masses about yourself on every level. You will know quite a lot about what makes you tick, both physically and mentally. You will probably have a more realistic image of yourself. You will know the effects of exercise on your body and what activities work best for you. You will understand what foods make you put on weight and how to adjust your diet accordingly.

Hopefully, you will be a happier person also. You will have restructured your life to suit your individual needs. Taking control in this way will have hopefully convinced you of your value as a human being. This is a very positive and powerful thing.

You are now a much healthier person as well. The possibility of you suffering from heart disease, diabetes, hypertension, strokes and arthritis is now greatly reduced. Your mobility has also increased, as being lighter and slimmer is allowing you to get around more easily. The pressure on your heart and lungs has been greatly reduced too, allowing lethargy and shortness of breath to be things of the past.

Let us not forget the wonderful sense of achievement that you should be feeling. You have solved a big problem that holds many people back from living their lives to the full. You are not only on your way to becoming a potential expert on what ought to be your most important subject, yourself, but you will also be a much wiser person, particularly about the planet.

This wisdom will continue to grow if you continue to eat whole foods. Stay away from chemicalised, dead, processed foods and you will not only stay slim, look great and be healthy, but you'll also become closer to your inner intuition and personal aspirations. Through this you will be able to move on to bigger and better things.

Don't be exploited by any of the many fast food chains. These massive organisations are making hundreds of millions of pounds by feeding you nutritionally deficient food. They don't have your self-interest in mind, only their own and it all comes down to money. Not only that, but many millions of animals are killed during the process. These types of foods are not only unhealthy but they will also make you overweight. Leave them alone if you want to stay slim.

It is without a doubt a very individual and subtle balance between what you can and can't eat and how much you can eat in relation to your body fat quantity. This will apply to your activity level as well. As an ex-sufferer of obesity or weight gain problems, you will know this all too well. The art is to keep this balance finely tuned to keep that fat away. The way to do this is to not allow yourself to get too hungry. Continue to nibble on food from the RIGHT food group. Also, keep active but don't exhaust yourself.

You will have to eat whole and natural foods for the rest of your life, but hey, I do that and I don't suffer from weight problems! If I can do it, so can you. There's nothing wrong with eating healthy. In fact, I would go so far as to say it's a wise thing to do. Whatever your reasons for eating natural foods, you can only benefit from them.

One thing to consider when combining diet and exercise is your carbohydrate intake. Carbohydrates are vital for energy. If you want to remain active and healthy, do not eat a diet deficient in these foods. For a quick boost of energy, eat snacks consisting of bananas, dates, raisins, sultanas, dried figs and/or dried apricots. These are known as simple carbohydrates as are other fruits, fresh or dried. They are absorbed by the body far quicker than complex carbohydrates, which consist of brown rice, wholemeal bread, pasta, cereals and vegetables. Complex carbohydrates provide a more steady flow of energy and for this reason, many athletes, especially long distance runners, eat a diet that is high in these foods.

When fruits are eaten, the fructose (fruit sugar) they contain provides a valuable source of energy, as well as a good supply of vitamins, minerals and fibre. This is not the case with another form of simple carbohydrate, sucrose, more commonly known as sugar. It gives us a quick boost but has no nutritional value. For this reason it is said to contain 'empty calories'.

So basically, eat plenty of complex and simple carbohydrates and cut right back on sugary foods that are totally deficient in nutrients, but very high in calories. You should be doing this anyway, but the point is you must continue if you want to remain slim. Fizzy drinks also contain high levels of sugar and should therefore be left alone.

Exercising regularly has many advantages.

*Walking:*

It's gentle and easy to fit into your life. It stimulates the heart, lungs, muscles and the mind. Studies have shown that even very little walking can prolong your life.

*Jogging:*

Helps to prevent a wide variety of health problems, including high blood pressure, high cholesterol levels and heart disease.

*Swimming:*

It works most of the major muscle groups and is an excellent aerobic exercise. It builds strength and stamina without putting stress on the joints and is an excellent exercise for people who are overweight, pregnant or unfit.

*Cycling:*

In my opinion is one of the best exercises for the body, along with swimming. It exercises the heart and lungs and builds stamina.

There are many other active sports or hobbies you can participate in to keep you interested in staying active. What about dancing? Ballroom for general mobility, tap or Irish for lower body strength, Latin American for strength and flexibility or barn dancing for aerobic exercise.

All of the previous different types of exercise will have similar effects on your respiration and heart rate. For that reason, they will all keep you fitter and healthier and hence less prone to health problems such as heart disease, high cholesterol levels and high blood pressure among others.

Apart from these similarities, they also all burn calories. This is quite helpful when you are trying to master the art of balancing your quality and quantity of food intake in relation to your energy expenditure. In simple terms, if you eat more food than your body uses up for energy, the surplus calories are stored on your body as fat. This simple fact applies to whatever type of food you are eating, unhealthy or not. But let's face it, if you're eating a high fat, high sugar diet, you've got to go some to keep it off. Therefore, it makes sense to eat a low fat, low sugar diet, balanced with an active lifestyle if you want to stay slim.

Don't forget the importance of getting enough rest and quality sleep. If you don't get the chance to rest during the day, then make sure you get to bed early. Not getting enough rest can deplete the body's store of nutrients and cause fatigue. For other reasons to get ample rest, *refer to Chapter 9 – EXERCISE, page 80.*

Relationships can also be a cause for concern. If you have a partner, husband or wife who is still how you used to be, overweight, it may cause problems. If you and this person used to eat and live the same way, but now you are slimmer, more active and generally living a different life, you may grow apart. Hopefully your partner etc. will understand and fully support you in whatever you do. However, many men and women become very insecure if their spouse is looking slim, attractive and generally happier. This is especially so if they are at home feeling overweight, unattractive and unhappy, while you are out enjoying yourself. You need to anticipate this and plan ahead.

Of course, ideally it would be great if the rest of your family, if you have children and a partner or spouse, came on your journey with you. The children might prove a little difficult, although we manage well enough. However, if the children are difficult to convert to a cleaner way of living, seeing their parents exercising and eating healthily together may help, although you will be up against the world as far as your children are concerned. This is because every other kid they come into contact with is eating this, that and the other. I know this all too well, but that doesn't stop me from trying. The whole point is I think it's worth it. The amount of additives children are consuming these days is frightening. Is this really what you want for your children's little clean bodies?

Don't force them, rather encourage and educate them about the possible effects these foods might have on their health. If they are overweight themselves, then they already have some idea. Introduce the cleaner foods to them slowly to allow them time to get accustomed to the different tastes. Reward them for eating cleaner in ways that they can relate to. If little Johnny loves football, take him for longer to the park if he manages to eat all his vegetables. If he can't, then maybe you shouldn't let him have that yoghurt that he loves so much.

At the end of the day, if you let your children eat what they wanted, it would be everything in sight. If you've got cupboards full of biscuits cakes and sweets etc, whether for you or not, you're not helping them. Don't kill your kids with kindness. If you are going to attempt to change your child's diet and lifestyle, do it gently and wisely.

I know a child who has suffered from asthma, eczema and hyperactivity. His parents have changed his diet gradually to a cleaner, additive free one and noticed improvement almost instantly. He is now a complete vegan. He doesn't eat any meat or any dairy products whatsoever. His asthma has greatly improved due to having less phlegm in his body, as dairy products cause phlegm and this aggravates asthma. He no longer suffers from eczema and he is much calmer. However, if he were to drink milk he would be covered in eczema almost instantly. He used to get annoyed with his body because he couldn't eat anything. His father told him that God gave him his body to remind him not to eat unhealthy foods, so he is lucky and can be proud of it because he will benefit in the long run from eating healthily.

He is now very used to his diet and I am told he enjoys it. One thing is for sure, he doesn't enjoy being covered in eczema. His parents don't like seeing him like it either. It is distressing to all of them. A certain amount of strictness is required with him as he is only seven years old and still finds it hard sometimes when kids at school are eating everything else. He is slowly accepting his physical problems and coming to terms with the fact that he can't eat what the other children eat. To tell you the truth, his parents don't want him eating what the other kids eat, because most of the time it's full of additives and nutritionally deficient. He is growing and needs an abundance of nutrients. A diet high in fruit and whole foods supplies him with everything he needs, without the added ingredients that affect his health.

Even if your child doesn't suffer from these types of health problems, look at what you are putting in their bodies. My point is, if you can all work on your lifestyle together as a family unit, you can all benefit whether overweight or not.

How to change your child's lifestyle or diet is beyond the scope of this book. Therefore, you may want to seek further help. Try the library or seek the advice of an holistic health practitioner, such as a naturopath or dietician.

For those of you that are free and single, the only hurdle between you and long-term health and a permanently slim body is yourself. You need to get yourself into a balanced way of life and a stable routine that works best for you.

Basically, if you want to remain slim and energetic, you need to live your life towards that purpose. On the other hand, if you want to be a couch potato and eat crisps, hamburgers, hot dogs, takeaways and everything else from the WRONG food group, your health and your body shape will reflect that lifestyle. It's your choice, make the RIGHT one.

# CHAPTER 12

## FRUIT

I have decided to devote a whole chapter to fruit and one day will devote a whole book to it. The reason for this is because I believe it is the ultimate food designed for man, not only to eat occasionally, but also to live on completely. This may seem a bit extreme to the average person, but let's take a look at the facts.

### Apples

Apples are probably the most common fruit available in Britain. As the old saying goes, "an apple a day keeps the doctor away". Unfortunately, you have to do a bit more than eat an apple a day to stay away from the doctor. However, they are a good source of vitamin C, which is an ANTIOXIDANT and helps to maintain the immune system.

### Apricots

Fresh, ripe apricots are high in fibre and are a good source of beta-carotene. Beta-carotene is the plant form of vitamin A. It is one of the ANTIOXIDANT nutrients that research has indicated to possibly help prevent degenerative illnesses such as cancer and heart disease. Dried apricots are considered to be one of the great health foods because they are a compact and convenient source of nutrients. They

131

are a useful source of iron, a good source of fibre and an excellent source of potassium. Though beware of sulphur dioxide (E220) a preservative very commonly used in treating dried apricots. This treatment produces substances that may trigger off asthma attacks in susceptible individuals. Read the ingredient lists on all foods or buy organic.

## Avocados

The avocado is a rich source of vitamin E, a good source of potassium, has useful amounts of vitamin B6 and also supplies vitamin C, riboflavin and manganese. It also has the highest protein content of any fruit. People say, if you are trying to lose weight, you should not eat avocados as they have a high fat content. Although this is largely true, it is not like eating fat that forms part of a meat dish or a fry-up. It is not refined oil such as cooking oil, where many thousands of olives have been pressed. It's a naturally occurring fat that can only be found in nature's complete package. Having said this, you wouldn't want to eat too many on a weight loss programme when eating other foods. However, on an all fruit diet, you will be able to eat as many as you feel you need to.

## Bananas

Bananas are, without a doubt, probably one of the most eaten fruits, especially by children. Healthy, filling, conveniently wrapped and tasty, they are one of nature's ideal snacks. They are high in potassium and easy to digest, though may cause constipation in certain individuals.

## Berries

There is an incredible variety of berries in existence throughout the world, from the well-known strawberry to the lesser known blueberry or gooseberry. They are all very good sources of vitamin C, especially blackcurrants and strawberries. Children happily eat them, though this will need to be done quickly as they don't keep for long once picked. Redcurrants are also a good source of potassium.

## Cherries

Raw cherries are a good source of potassium and contain useful amounts of vitamin C. They are very cleansing and detoxifying and believed to cleanse the kidneys. They are a mild laxative and therefore help to relieve constipation. 225g (8 oz) of cherries eaten daily will lower levels of uric acid in the blood, which may help to prevent gout.

## Dates

Dates are an incredible fruit, packed with nourishment. A 100g (3½ oz portion of fresh dates provides 107 calories. The same weight of dried dates contains 227 calories. Fresh dates are the better source of vitamin C with a 100g serving providing nearly a third of the recommended daily intake. They are also a useful source of soluble fibre, making them a gentle laxative without irritating the bowel or stomach. Dried dates are a more concentrated source of nutrients than fresh ones, being higher in calcium, potassium, niacin, copper, iron, magnesium and folic acid.

### Figs

Dried figs contain roughly six times as many calories as fresh ones. Drying also concentrates the nutrients, making them a rich source of potassium and a useful source of calcium, iron, magnesium, carotene and vitamin C. They also contain dietary fibre.

### Grapefruit

These are a rich source of vitamin C, with half a fruit providing more than half of the adult daily requirement. They also contain a useful amount of pectin, a form of soluble fibre that may help to lower levels of blood cholesterol. It also contains potassium, as well as being low in calories.

### Grapes

Grapes are a good source of potassium. They also contain vitamin C, though in small amounts. Black and red grapes are high in ANTIOXIDANTS, which are thought to neutralise FREE RADICALS. This may help to protect the body against cancer and heart disease.

### Guava

Weight for weight, the guava contains more than five times as much vitamin C as an orange. Vitamin C is vital for the production of collagen, as well as healthy skin and tissues. It is also an ANTIOXIDANT, helpful in mopping up potentially harmful FREE RADICALS. The flesh and seeds of the guava are a useful source of soluble fibre in the form of pectin. The fruit is also a good source of potassium, which may assist in regulating blood pressure.

## Kiwi

The kiwi fruit originally came from China and used to be known as the Chinese gooseberry. It is an excellent source of vitamin C, a good source of potassium and supplies useful amounts of soluble fibre.

## Lemons

Lemons are high in vitamin C and are also very cleansing, as all fruits are, especially citrus. Hot water with a freshly squeezed lemon, drunk on an empty stomach first thing in the morning, is very helpful in relieving constipation, as well as cleansing the liver and colon.

## Mangoes

A medium sized mango is a rich source of both beta-carotene, as well as vitamin C. The flesh of the mango is easy to digest and the beta-carotene it contains is readily absorbed where it can be converted into vitamin A. Vitamin C and beta-carotene are ANTIOXIDANTS. Antioxidants supplied by food boost defences and help to prevent FREE

RADICAL damage, thereby reducing the risk of certain cancers. The mango is also high in sugars and will give the body a boost of energy.

### Melons

Of all the melons, the orange fleshed cantaloupe melon is probably the most nutritious. High in vitamin C and a good source of beta-carotene, they also provide dietary fibre, sugars, potassium, sulphur and folic acid.

### Nectarines

A variety of peach with a smooth skin that, just like the peach is rich in vitamin C. They also contain sugars, dietary fibre and beta-carotene.

### Oranges

Oranges are probably most associated with vitamin C and quite rightly so. Just one medium sized fruit supplies more than the adult daily requirement, but that's not all they contain. They also provide sugars, dietary fibre, folic acid, pectin and two of the B vitamins, thiamine and folate. The membranes of the fruit also contain bioflavonoids, which have antioxidant properties. What a wonderful food.

### Papaya

Also known as a paw paw, this tropical fruit is an excellent source of vitamin C and a good source of beta-carotene. It also provides sugars, dietary fibre and small amounts of calcium and iron.

## Passion Fruit

Passion fruit is high in dietary fibre and also provides sugars, vitamin C, potassium, magnesium and phosphorus.

## Peaches

Peaches are a rich source of vitamin C, as well as providing sugars, carotene, niacin and potassium. Dried peaches also contain iron, providing two fifths of the adult daily requirements from a 50g (1¾ oz) serving.

## Pears

Pears are high in natural fruit sugars, providing you with a quick and convenient source of energy. They also provide dietary fibre in the form of pectin, as well as vitamin C. Dried pears contain iron and are rich in potassium.

## Pineapples

Once again, vitamin C is the main nutrient, with natural fruit sugars, potassium, magnesium and dietary fibre also being provided.

## Plums

There are a great variety of plums, around 2,000 in all. They contain vitamin E, vitamin C, potassium, carotene, natural fruit sugars and dietary fibre. Dried plums (prunes) are a more concentrated source of nutrients, especially potassium and iron. They also contain vitamin B6.

## Raisins

These dried, black, seedless grapes are high in natural sugars, making them a very good source of energy. Though high in calories, they are low in fat so can be eaten by people trying to lose weight. This applies to all fruits, even dates, though the principle of eating in moderation should be applied. Raisins are high in potassium and dietary fibre. They also provide iron, calcium, magnesium and other micronutrients.

## Satsumas

Belonging to the same group as tangerines, mandarins and clementines, they have pretty much the same nutrient content. They are a good source of vitamin C and also provide carotene, folic acid and dietary fibre. The membrane and pith also contain bioflavonoids, which act like antioxidants.

Having read the above information, you can probably understand how I find it interesting, if not frustrating when people think and say to me, that living on a pure fruit diet will leave you deficient in some way. The people that think or say this are usually consuming a diet of dead, nutritionally deficient food themselves without realising it.

Not every vitamin and mineral is present in an all fruit diet, but what it lacks in some vitamins and minerals, it more than makes up for in live enzymes and 'life force' (aliveness). It is a natural living food that the body will benefit from immensely. You can consume all the vitamins and minerals you want, but if your body isn't capable of absorbing them, there really isn't much point. This is the problem for most people, due to unclean bodies and deficient or weak digestive systems.

Fruit is easily digested and absorbed by the body. It is low in fat and is also very cleansing. It is an ideal food for health, as well as losing weight. Don't be misguided by people who tell you that fruit is high in calories and therefore fattening. Yes, it is high in naturally occurring sugars, but fattening? Not a chance. I sometimes spend months on fruit alone and eat large quantities every day, yet people tell me how slim or even skinny I am.

Some people believe that fruit gives them diarrhoea. This is a misconception. This reaction is due to the fruit doing its job of internal cleansing. Did you know that the average individual (practically everybody) is carrying around six to twelve pounds of uneliminated faeces. Not a very nice thought is it? Don't think for a minute that passing motion once, twice or even three times a day gets you off the hook, it doesn't. The pockets of the large intestine are holding on to this waste material and the body is continuously re-absorbing the toxins and poisons that are produced there. Eating fruit, with its cleansing and laxative properties, loosens this uneliminated material and diarrhoea is usually the result.

Fruit is a valuable source of ANTIOXIDANTS. These antioxidants are vital in protecting the body against numerous infections, including certain cancers and heart diseases. They do this by neutralising FREE RADICALS. Free radicals are chemicals that are produced in the body as part of its metabolism and defence against infections. Free radical production is increased when the body is exposed to excessive environmental pollution or illness. Unfortunately, free radicals are potentially harmful if left unchecked and create conditions that may cause heart disease, cancer, infections and various illnesses.

The more free radicals that are present in our body, the more antioxidants are required to neutralise them. In today's high pollutant society, most everybody is producing high amounts of free radicals. It is true that the body produces its own antioxidants, but it also relies largely on food sources. Vitamin E and C, beta-carotene, selenium and bioflavonoids all help to neutralise free radicals and their effects. These nutrients with their antioxidant properties, are found in many if not most fruits.

### Caution

Fruit is extremely cleansing and if the toxins and poisons in your body are loosened too rapidly through a fruit diet, it may overload your system. This could be dangerous to your health. Therefore, fruit should be slowly introduced and gradually increased over a period of time to minimise this risk.

# CHAPTER 13

# FASTING FOR HEALTH AND WEIGHT LOSS

Fasting is without a doubt, the oldest and most natural form of medicine available to man. Unfortunately, it doesn't get used very often. If it was practised more regularly, I believe there would be fewer diseases in the world today.

Have you ever thought why your appetite diminishes whenever you are unwell? What is the first thing your dog or any other animal does when it gets ill? IT STOPS EATING! What does this tell you? I don't know about you, but it tells me that my body or the body in question, be it an animal's or a human's, is somehow trying to cure itself of its diseased situation through fasting. Therefore, would it be reasonable to assume that physical bodies, human or otherwise, have an in-built mechanism for cleansing themselves, providing they are given the chance.

Nature is both complex and at the same time, fantastically simple. It works in such subtle and sometimes mysterious ways, that even modern science looks on in bewilderment. Our bodies are natural healers. Without obstacles (food) in the way, they are designed to automatically restore health and vitality through the elimination of toxins and poisons that may have been there for years.

Today's modern society is overflowing with food. How many programmes are shown on television about cooking? I've lost count! There are so many different types of cuisine available, either to take away or sit down to, that you could almost go around the world on food in your local high street. We eat for any occasion and make so much fuss about food, that we not only forget that food is primarily fuel, but we also forget the importance of *not* eating. The relationship between food or no food as it were, and health, has been lost due to today's fast-paced lifestyle and the fact that we tend to eat for social and entertaining reasons, instead of concentrating on what our body actually requires. This ultimately results in overeating.

We are supposedly progressing as a species, yet still find ourselves plagued by a very long list of common ailments and diseases. Many of these are fatal and most of which modern medicine cannot cure without some kind of operation. Even then, it may not be permanent.

Fifty or sixty years ago, health problems and diseases like high blood pressure, heart disease, arteriosclerosis and lung and colon cancer were not prevalent. So why are they so common now? It can only be due to our lifestyles, what we eat and global pollution. These three factors have a positive or negative effect on the body. Actually, global pollution can only and does have a negative effect on the physical body as far as I am aware. The other two factors as stated can be positive or negative depending on (a) how you live, and (b) what you eat.

The whole point is, even if you are eating really well, as I hope you are by now, the need to detoxify further is just as important. As previously mentioned, the average individual (by this I mean practically everybody) is walking around with anything from 6-10 pounds of uneliminated faeces! This simple fact still applies to an individual whose diet consists of foods from the RIGHT food group, as outlined in this book. The pockets of the large intestine to a greater or lesser degree, harbour old faeces from years back. Passing motion two or three times a day means nothing when you continue to push food into your mouth at such an alarming rate. The walls of the colon (large intestine) never get a chance to clean themselves. This fact can be likened to a water pipe that still allows water through, even though it may be greatly furred up. Continually carrying this mass of filthy uneliminated matter around throughout an individual's life, must surely be detrimental to health. The poisonous toxins that form there are continuously reabsorbed back into circulation, thereby poisoning the bloodstream, which feeds every organ, gland and cell.

As you now know, our diets are full of toxins in the form of colours, flavours, preservatives, pesticides, herbicides and other indigestible substances. Our bodies are limited in their ability to store and/or eliminate these toxins. A diet high in these substances overloads our kidneys, liver, lungs, bowels and skin. As this overload accumulates from years of incorrect eating, as well as environmental pollution, elimination and normal functioning become impaired. Many people and natural hygienists believe that this build-up of toxins from diet, as well as the build-up of faecal matter in the colon, is the cause of all diseases. I'm inclined to agree.

The principle behind fasting is simple, restored health through cleansing. Essentially, fasting promotes health by giving the body a chance to cast off poisons. It is more of an opportunity for rejuvenation than it is a cure. The great thing about it is the fact that it is so wonderfully simple. It is the practice of abstinence. Refraining from eating, to allow your body's natural healing powers to come into play.

I realise that many of you will be thinking that a lot of what I am saying about fasting contradicts many of the principles outlined in this book. Particularly the fact that I have told you to eat plenty of food and here I am saying that we all eat too much. You must understand that this book is primarily about losing weight and in order to do that you need to speed up your metabolism and at the same time strengthen the liver with adequate nutrients. Also by eating in this manner, you can slowly start to detoxify without putting your health at risk. Of course you would lose weight through fasting, but it might also be dangerous to your health due to the toxins being loosened too rapidly.

By eating in the way that this book suggests, you will have prepared yourself physically, to take up short fasts of a day or so if you wish. The cleaner you are internally, the longer you can go without food. On the other hand, the more toxins and poisons that your body is harbouring, the more unpleasant your fast will be.

To cut this unpleasantness down, all you have to do is eat cleaner on the days building up to a fast. In this way your body detoxifies at a faster rate. If you have already laid the foundation to detoxify quicker by only eating the foods from the RIGHT food group, you will be fine when you take it a step further by eating cleaner.

Many people say it is dangerous and that you shouldn't fast. However, their perspective has become distorted due to their fear through lack of knowledge. It is an old cure that still works, even for modern problems caused by today's excessive lifestyles. It's such a shame that this simple yet powerful healing method is so ignored.

Many different types of people and religions have used fasting throughout time. Moses, Elijah and Jesus all fasted for up to forty days. Jews to this day fast. Moslems during Ramadan, Christians during lent and Hindus fast routinely.

## Ailments traditionally treated with fasting

Acne
Arteriosclerosis
Asthma
Boils
Bronchitis
Constipation
Diarrhoea
Gall Stones
Hay Fever
High Blood Pressure

Hives
Inflammations
Insomnia
Liver Problems
Migraine
Obesity
Psoriasis
Rheumatism
Tumours
Ulcers

Even if you don't suffer from any of the above, periodic fasting can be a preventative measure rather than a cure. However, if you are reading this book, it will be due to the fact that you suffer from weight gain problems. Fasting is probably the most rewarding of all the weight loss diets as the results are quick.

## Weight Loss

During a fast the body still requires energy for normal functions. It takes it from the most available source second to food. It uses fat reserves first and muscle tissues from various parts of the body last. An obese person can lose up to 65% of his/her body weight in this way. When fat resources are depleted, true hunger returns (not false hunger like most of us are subject to) and it is time to start eating. However, I have heard of obese people fasting for six days or more and not losing any weight. I believe this is due to the fact that their livers are not healthy enough to Metabolise their fat reserves. For this reason and reasons previously mentioned, YOU MUST EAT YOURSELF INTO THE RIGHT CONDITION TO FAST SAFELY AND TO BENEFIT FROM THAT FAST. For many of you, it may mean at least a year on the RIGHT foods outlined in this book, before it is safe to fast for any real length of time. However, if you have been eating the RIGHT foods for at least six months, then you can start with short fasts and build up slowly from there.

Have you ever thought why it is, that in the morning you wake and feel a little rough until you eat or drink something? During the night, if you didn't eat too late, your body is starting to detoxify, as you don't eat while you are asleep. In effect, during the night you are fasting. Take a look at your tongue in the mirror first thing in the morning. I'll take a guess and say it has got fur or a greasy coating of some kind on its surface. This is an indication that the body is trying to rid itself of internal mucus and toxins. The Chinese use the tongue as a major tool of diagnosis in their medicine as do other long standing proven methods of Eastern medicine. After you have eaten your breakfast, take another look at your tongue. I'll bet the coating has more or less disappeared. The body now concentrating on digestion, stops deep cleansing. You feel better as well probably. This is because when the body starts to detoxify at a faster rate as when not eating, toxins pour into the bloodstream. These toxins make us feel bad as they are impure and unclean. It is said that toxins hurt us twice, once on the way in and once on the way out. When we eat, this process of toxin elimination ceases. Therefore, we feel better. In our ignorance, we think that we feel bad due to the lack of food. How wrong we are. It is due to too much food, usually of the wrong kind and the effects of their impurities.

## The Morning Fast

I personally know people who feel ill if they miss their breakfast. This is not a good sign. This indicates that their body is overloaded with toxins and they need to detoxify. Start to miss your breakfast and see how you feel. Drink the drink you are accustomed to and plenty of water or juice if you get a headache, which may happen. It is likely that you might get a harmless sensation of some kind for the first 1-3 days of this practice. After that, you should feel much better, work better and enjoy your lunch more than ever. Keep this up indefinitely, it is a healthy practice. I never eat breakfast and if I do, it consists of fruit only. I am very rarely ill and I manage to work quite a lot and have enough energy for past-time ventures as well as a family.

If you find that cutting out your breakfast makes you feel ill, then go back to the RIGHT food group and give up meat also. You have to ask yourself what is more important, the taste of some poor dead animal's leg or your health? Stick with vegetarianism for a month or so and try again. Slowly, over a period of time, refine your diet down cleaner and cleaner. Vegetarian to vegan (no dairy). This can take time, so be patient.

## The 24-hour Fast

This is obviously the next step on from missing your breakfast. You must be able to comfortably miss your breakfast before going without food for a whole day. If you can't, then 24 hours will be even more unpleasant. A good test is to eat fruit only for a whole day and nothing else. To take it one step further would be to eat just one type of fruit for a whole day. A day of grapes for example, would be extremely detoxifying, whilst still having the benefits of solid food. In fact, if you were to do this, just eat fruit for a whole day, once, twice or three times a week, you would benefit immensely. Start slowly with this though, as with everything else in this book. See how you feel and build up gradually. Don't be scared, just take your time and you will be fine.

In a study on mice who were fasted every third day, their life span was increased by 40%. This is the equivalent to two days of fasting every six days or almost a week. If you were to practice one day of fasting every week, it is quite possible that you could increase your life span by 20%, and let's not forget the amount of weight that you could also be losing! You can benefit in many ways from fasting if you eat yourself into the right condition to try it.

## The Pre-fast Diet

The purpose of the pre-fast diet is to prepare you physically and mentally for the aggressive detoxification of the fast. As already mentioned, fruit would serve this purpose well. The length of time that the pre-fast diet will last, is determined by the possible length of the fast itself. I say possible length because unless you are experienced, it is difficult to say exactly how long you are going to be fasting for. To be honest, it is still quite difficult even when you are relatively experienced, although you will have more of an idea.

Let us say you wanted to fast on Sunday. Because it is just a one day fast, not quite as much preparation is necessary as for fasts of a longer duration. You may want to eat salads and fruit (separately), along with fruit juices and/or vegetable juices on Friday. On Saturday just fruits and fruit juices. You may experience some detoxification symptoms just from the pre-fast diet itself. If it is too much for you, then break it by eating some of your usual foods. You may have to do this for a number of weeks before you can actually fast for a whole day. By the way, when I say usual foods, I mean from the RIGHT food group, not your old foods.

So basically you have to eat cleaner and cleaner until you are able to fast. A one-day fast shouldn't be too difficult for you if you have been eating the RIGHT foods for the last six months.

### What to Expect During a Fast

Generally speaking, you may experience bad breath, body odour, fatigue/exhaustion, nausea, shortness of breath, general aching, anxiety, diarrhoea and/or skin eruptions. For a one-day fast, these symptoms are pretty unlikely, although you will probably experience mild bouts of some of them. Basically, your body is battling with the toxins whatever they are. They could be anything – colours, flavours, preservatives, prescription drugs, social drugs, pesticides and/or herbicides. Unfortunately, this is a natural process of detoxification. If you want these poisons out of your body, you have to make some kind of sacrifice for all the WRONG foods that you've consumed. A little discomfort is a small price to pay for all the wrong that you have done to your body.

Of course, if it becomes too unpleasant, break the fast by eating some food from the RIGHT food group. I doubt if it will get too unpleasant on a one-day fast though.

### Drinks Whilst you are Fasting

There are many different types of fasts. Fruit juice, vegetable juice, water and even a milk fast, to name but a few. Basically, they are all restricting the amount of nourishment that you are taking in, so as to allow your body that valuable time to cleanse and heal itself. The most aggressive type of fast is the pure water fast. You must be experienced to embark on a fast of this nature. Second to this is the fruit juice and then the vegetable juice. The milk fast is more of a camouflage fast than anything else. Although I have heard reports of a woman who lost quite a lot of weight using this method over a number of weeks.

During your one-day fast, drink as much fruit or vegetable juice as you like. This will curb your hunger, as well as slow the detox down a little, making it a bit easier. Prune juice is a good thing to drink on a fast for obvious reasons. It loosens the contents of the bowels, thus aiding detoxification.

## Rest

On your fasting day, make sure you take it easy. Lay around all day if you have to. For this reason, you should choose a day for your fast with this in mind. Your body will be going through a lot of chemical changes and will want as much energy as it can get to do its house cleaning. Don't waste that energy elsewhere by doing something strenuous. Rest!

## Breaking the Fast

If you started your fast at 6 p.m. Saturday night, you should break it at 6 p.m. Sunday night, with a meal of fruits or a light salad. Resume normal eating the following day after a light breakfast, say of fruits.

If you were to practice this once a week or even every two weeks, your health would increase significantly, whilst your body weight did the exact opposite (decrease significantly).

I am not going to take you any further than this, as it is beyond the scope of this book. Quite honestly, I have only touched the surface as far as fasting is concerned. If you want to learn more and possibly build up to the longer fasts, vital for deeper, cellular cleansing, then further reading will be necessary. A short list can be found towards the back of this book.

## Non-food for thought

Imagine a tablet that could cleanse and strengthen your body, revitalise your spirit, clear your mind and even make you lose weight. Wow! That tablet would sell, I'm sure, at any price. Fasting does all of these things, yet it doesn't sell even though it is free. Why? Basically, fasting means taking your health into your own hands. To most people this is scary. Fasting requires courage, willpower, confidence and knowledge. However, these things grow with experience. The more you fast the easier it will become. There are people who live such clean lives, that they miss eating for a day here or two days there, without even realising it.

Make fasting a part of your overall plan for a slimmer, healthier body and you will, without a shadow of a doubt, benefit immensely.

# SUMMARY

"You are what you eat". This must be one of the truest statements ever made. Most people aren't born ill, it happens over a period of time. Therefore, it has to come from somewhere outside the body. As time goes by, we continuously fill our bodies with dead, processed foods that not only lack nutrients, but also contain many additives. These have a slow but definite effect on our bodies, and health slips away.

For the overweight individual, the principle is exactly the same. If you eat a high fat, high toxin diet, then you will be a high fat, high toxin person. This obviously has consequences in more ways than one, least not your health!

FOOD IS FOR FUEL NOT FUN. Don't be a slave to your tongue. Of course, we have to enjoy our food or we couldn't eat it. However, don't eat more than you need and only eat healthily, whole foods and fruit. Eating natural foods will bring improvement to both your physical and mental health.

New bodies aren't created overnight. This type of transformation can take years of hard work. Anything worth having doesn't come easy, so you have to fight for it. Food is an addiction to many people and if you are one of them, you must learn to change your outlook if you haven't already done so.

"A journey of a thousand miles starts with but a single step"! (Chinese proverb) - Take that step. Good luck!

# FURTHER READING

**Arnold Ehret:** *Mucusless Diet Healing System.*
Ehret Literature Publishing Co. Inc. 1953

**Arnold Ehret:** *Rational Fasting: For Physical, Mental and Spiritual Rejuvenation.* Ehret Literature Publishing Co. Inc. 1966, 1987, 1994. ISBN 1-884772-01-3

**Aveline Kushi:** *Complete Guide to Macrobiotic Cooking.* Warner Books 1985. ISBN 0-446-38634-0

**Chee Soo:** *The Chinese Art of T'ai Chi Ch'uan. The Taoist Way to Mental and Physical Health.* The Aquarian Press 1984. ISBN O-85030-387-7

**Essie Honiball:** *I Live On Fruit.* Benedic Books 1989. ISBN 0-86812-231-9

**Master Lam Kam Chuen:** *The Way of Energy. Mastering the Chinese Art of Internal Strength with Chi Kung Exercise.* Gala Books Ltd 1991. ISBN 1-85675-020-5

**Readers Digest:** *Foods That Harm, Foods That Heal. An A-Z Guide to Safe and Healthy Eating.* The Readers Digest Association Ltd London 1996. ISBN 0-276-421930

**Rejean Durette:** *Fruit: The Ultimate Diet.* Fruitarian Vibes 1999. Available from Fresh Network.

**Steve Meyerowitz:** *Juice Fasting & Detoxification.* Book Publishing Company. ISBN 1-878736-65-5

# Useful Organisations

**Alcohol Concern:** Waterbridge House, 32-36 Loman Street, London SE1 0EE. Tel: 0207-928-7377.

**Arthritic Association:** First Floor Suite, 2 Hyde Gardens, Eastbourne, East Sussex BN21 4PN Tel: 01323-416550 or 0207-491-0233

**British Acupuncture Council:** 63 Jeddo Road, London, W12 9HQ. Tel: 0208-735-0400

**British Allergy Foundation:** St Bartholomew's Hospital, West Smithfield, London EC1A 7BE Tel: 0207-600-6166

**British College of Naturopathy and Osteopathy:** 6 Netherhall Gardens, London NW3 5RR Tel: 0207-435-6464

**British Heart Foundation:** 14 Fitzhardinge Street, London W1H 6DH  Tel: 0207-935-0185

**British Herbal Medicine Association:** Sun House, Church Street, Stroud, Gloucestershire GL5 1JL Tel: 01453-751-389

**British Nutrition Foundation:** High Holborn House, 52-54 High Holborn, London WC1V 6RQ Tel: 0207-404-6504

**British School of Yoga:** Stanhope Square, Holsworthy, Devon EX22 6DF Tel: 0800-7319271

**Department of Health:** Richmond House, 79 Whitehall, London SW1A 2NS Tel: 0207-210-3000

**NHS Smokers Helpline:** Tel: 0800-1690169

**Quit (Smoking):** 211 Old Street, London EC1V 9NR Tel: 0800-002200

**Royal London Homeopathic Hospital:** 60 Great Ormond Street, London WC1N 3HR. Tel: 0207-837-8833

**The Fresh Network:** Fruitarian and Raw Energy Support & Help, P.O. Box 71, Ely, Cambs. CB7 4GU Tel: 01353-662849